Napoleon

Napoleon

Timothy Wilson Smith

HAUS PUBLISHING · LONDON

First published in Great Britain in 2007 by
Haus Publishing Limited
26 Cadogan Court
Draycott Avenue
London SW3 3BX

www.hauspublishing.co.uk

Copyright © The estate of Timothy Wilson Smith, 2007

The moral right of the author has been asserted

A CIP catalogue record for this book is available from the British Library

ISBN 978-1-904950-26-4

Typeset in Garamond 3 by MacGuru Ltd
info@macguru.org.uk

Printed in Dubai by Oriental Press

Front cover: *Napoleon on the Imperial Throne* by J A D Ingres (1806) courtesy
akg Images

Contents

For Pam, Bonapartist

Corsican boy-soldier 1769–85

Letizia Ramolino (1750–1836) was a devout and dutiful young Catholic girl living in her hometown of Ajaccio in Corsica. Her family, which came originally from Lombardy in northern Italy, and her dowry of 31 acres, which included a mill and a bread-making oven, were attractive enough to catch the attention of a minor local nobleman, Carlo Buonaparte (1746–85). An ambitious young lawyer, whose family claimed origins in Tuscany, Buonaparte himself owned two vineyards as well as some pasture and arable land. The two were married when Letizia was only 14 and she came to live in a spacious house with her husband, his mother, his uncle the archdeacon of Ajaccio and some cousins. As her father had died when she was five, her stepfather, a Swiss soldier named Captain Fesch, who recently had fathered her half-brother, Giuseppe (later Joseph, 1763–1839), gave her away at her wedding.

Eventually the marriage was to prove fertile, but the young couple lost their first two children before they kept the third, another Giuseppe (later Joseph, 1768–1844). Now at the hottest time of the next year Letizia was expecting her second child. On 15 August, the Feast of the Assumption, she went to mass at the cathedral of Ajaccio but had to leave the church in a hurry as her contractions began. Her sister-in-law, Geltruda Paravicini, helped her back to the family home just a short distance away, but Letizia could not reach the bedroom in time and her second son was

Napoleon's mother, Letizia Bonaparte – Madame Mère

born on a couch on the ground floor. He was called Nabulione or Napoleone after both an obscure Greek saint and a close relative.

It was to be several years before Letizia had more children but then they arrived as if on a steady conveyor belt. First came Lucciano (Lucien, 1775–1840), and Maria Anna Elisa (Elise, 1777–1820) then Luigi (Louis, 1778–1846), and at regular intervals Paolina (Pauline, 1780–1825), Carolina (Caroline, 1782–1839) and Girolamo (Jérôme, 1784–1860). In the end Letizia had 13 children and she could count herself lucky that eight of them survived. They were given Italian names as they were born Corsicans to parents who emphasised that they were of Italian stock, but they came to use French versions of those names because their island became part of France and it was in France that they made their fortunes.

Corsica found it hard to resist being dominated by one or other of the maritime city-states of western Italy. From the 14th century it had been in the orbit of Genoa, a city that devoted itself to banking; and Corsica came to be seen as an investment of Genoa's

Bank of St George. This was not how the Corsicans viewed themselves. Like other impoverished and bellicose people such as the Swiss, Scots and the Irish, they often made lucrative careers as guards for foreign rulers. One such soldier, who had been in the service of the King of Naples, was Pasquale Paoli (1725–1807). After Paoli returned to the island in 1755, he used his military training to mount a guerrilla campaign in the mountains to expel the Genoese and he succeeded in confining them to larger cities like Bastia and Ajaccio. His exploits made him famous throughout Europe.

At first the Bonapartes were sympathetic to Paoli's call for independence and around 1766–7 Carlo went to Rome to plead the island's cause with the Pope. Everything changed in 1768, when Genoa sold the island to France, and the struggle for independence inevitably became caught up in France's conflict with Britain for control of the western Mediterranean. France had just lost Minorca and wanted Corsica instead. By 1769 the Bonapartes had decided it was better to be on the winning side and had thrown in their lot with France. While Letizia was pregnant with Napoleon, she and her husband moved out of an area controlled by the Paolistas and went back to the French-controlled city of Ajaccio.

The dominant personality in Napoleon's family was his mother, who later bore the title of Madame Mère (Mrs Mother). She was always forceful and often harsh; she hated Napoleon's or anyone's lies; she was not overawed by her second son's success; she had no time for women she regarded as self-indulgent (like his first wife Joséphine); and she approved of men who, like him, took risks. Throughout Napoleon's childhood his father Carlo was preoccupied with status. He fought and won a case to increase the dowry his wife had received; he tried to win back family land that had been given away generations ago; and, now that the French ruled, he was quick to try to show that he was by birth an aristocrat, since nobility would exempt him from certain taxes and open up opportunities for his family. When Louis XVI (1754–93) became King of France, Carlo was chosen to be one of three who presented the island's compliments to their new sovereign.

It was perhaps during Carlo's absences that Letizia came to be close to the French governor of the island, Charles René, Comte de Marbeuf (1712–86). Some have maintained that she became his mistress and that her fourth son, Luigi, may have been his. Nothing is certain, except that Marbeuf took both a liking to Letizia and a keen interest in the family's affairs. In 1776 or 1777, Marbeuf told Carlo that he could do something for his oldest sons.

Hitherto Napoleon had been brought up in Ajaccio by nuns, then by priests, and despite family consciousness of their superior situation he played with any children in the neighbourhood, on condition that he won every game. His brother Joseph later told a story of how in a game of Carthaginians and Romans, the equivalent of Cowboys and Indians, Napoleon was once cast as a Carthaginian but refused to play until he was allowed to be a Roman, for he knew that the Romans must ultimately win. As a small boy he was belligerent. He would use any ruse in order to defeat his companions.

Marbeuf made an attractive proposal. As Joseph, Napoleon and Elise were noble but relatively impoverished, they could gain scholarships to continue their education in France. Provided that their claims to nobility were accepted, there would be no obstacle to their entrance into important schools. Joseph, who was quiet, would train for the priesthood, while Napoleon, who had to be directed to some kind of military career, would go to a recently established school in Champagne. Later Elise would board at St-Cyr, a school for young ladies. Marbeuf had already dealt directly with the Minister of War. Now all depended on the researches of a royal herald into the Bonapartes' family tree. Eventually the necessary caste distinction was uncovered. Provided that the boys could pass the entrance exams to their chosen institutions, the way ahead for them was clear.

In December 1778 a gaggle of Bonapartes left for the mainland. Carlo was on his way to Versailles to represent the Corsican Estates (political assembly) to the King. Joseph Fesch (1763–1839), Letizia's half-brother and therefore a Bonaparte by extension, was on his way to a seminary in Aix-en-Provence. Letizia's cousin, abbé Varèse, was leaving for Autun, where he had been appointed a subdeacon. The two boys were also going to Autun, there to learn French and to prepare for their entrance exams. The family may have been insignificant as they moved into the wider world of one of the greatest of European nations, but by going to France they were making sure that they could arrive. In *ancien régime* France a career was open to a man of noble birth. It would take Napoleon's success to open a career to any man with talent.

Since 987 France had been governed by kings, and had grown to become the largest and most populous country in western Europe by gradually gaining control of most of the lands north of the Pyrenees, west of the Alps and south-west of the Rhine. This piecemeal process of acquisition was reflected in its legal system, which included a dozen superior courts, in its system of taxation, which varied from area to area, and in its administration, in which areas called généralités, run by professional civil servants, cut across ancient provinces. The King was in theory an absolute monarch restrained only by some fundamental laws. He could make peace or war, imprison at will and appoint whomever he liked to advise or represent him. In practice the King was much less free to do what he liked. He had to respect privileges, above all those of the church and the nobility, the first two orders of the realm. Nevertheless, since 1614 no King had called the Estates General, a national body that the King could consult.

Louis XV, shy and idle, had been dominated by his famous mistress Madame de Pompadour (1721–64), whose 'reign' as official mistress had culminated in the unsuccessful Seven Years war (1756–63), in which France lost Canada to England and suffered naval and military defeats in Europe. But before her death La Pompadour had recommended the services of the vigorous Etienne, duc de Choiseul (1719–85). Choiseul's rebuilding of the army and navy and his scheme to annex Corsica would decisively affect the prospects of the young Napoleon Bonaparte.

Louis XV's untried successor and grandson, Louis XVI, profited from Choiseul's reforms; his minister of war Claude, comte de Saint-Germain (1707–78), made the army more professional, founded 12 provincial military schools to raise the standard of recruits and resumed the reform of the artillery that Choiseul had started. The new air of purpose was quickly evident in the course of the war France was fighting when Napoleon arrived in France. In 1777 as an ally of the rebellious American colonists Louis XVI had declared war on England and in 1781 at Yorktown in Virginia, while a French fleet prevented retreat by sea, an army that was as much French as it was American forced the British to surrender; and in 1783 at a conference in Paris the British had to concede the colonists their independence. As the British were fighting 3,000 miles from home, logistics probably made their defeat inevitable, but French assistance made what was probable certain. France was once more a formidable enemy on land and sea.

When little Napoleone Buonaparte arrived in France in 1778, what worried him was the fact that he was not French and that he had no French; and yet, though Napoleon had little gift for languages and always made mistakes in spoken French, he had soon learnt enough in Autun to be sent to military school. Joseph, who was to continue his education in Autun, cried openly when they parted; Napoleon brushed away a single tear.

When he arrived at the college of Brienne in May 1778, Napoleon needed to be tough. The comte de Saint-Germain's new school was a military establishment only in name. Though it had replaced an institution run by Franciscan friars, the friars were still in charge, and the regime was harsh. The fathers also had no idea how to prepare boys to become soldiers, except for eventually offering a course on fortification. Napoleon probably learnt more from reading the works of Julius Caesar. The curriculum was a standard one for the time. In the morning the boys studied Latin, a little German, mathematics, history, geography and drawing. The afternoons were given over to gentlemanly accomplishments such as fencing, dancing, music and handwriting. Napoleon hated the afternoons, for he was physically awkward, but he enjoyed history, which was about France's past victories, and geography, as he liked poring over maps, and he loved mathematics.

The boys wore uniform, their linen was changed twice a week, their days were regimented, food varied only on feast days and at night the boys were locked into their cells, which were six feet square. The authorities tried hard to stamp out homosexual encounters, without much success, it seems, and in his early days Napoleon suffered because he was unwilling to play the part of a 'nymph'. His resistance may have added to the taunting he received for his foreign looks, his Corsican origin and his odd Christian name, which they converted to 'paille au nez' (straw nose).

The silent movie *Napoléon* (1927) by Abel Gance (1889–1981) is a propaganda masterpiece. Its 330 minutes move from snowball fights at Brienne to campaigning in Italy. Among striking images are the lonely child's love of an eagle, the adult refugee sailing solo from Corsica and a split screen re-enactment of war.

Whenever Napoleon was around there were going to be fights. Though his parents had pragmatically pledged their allegiance to France, Napoleon was now, and would remain for many years to come, deeply divided in his feelings about Corsica. His accent alone showed where he had come from, so he made a point of being Corsican. He vehemently defended Paoli (who was in exile) and promised to join him in fighting for Corsica's independence. When the son of the French governor of Bastia (the main port of Corsica) arrived, he was persuaded to pretend he was Genoese and Napoleon at once attacked the boy. He was too proud to appeal for help to the masters and, though he was not liked, he slowly gained his contemporaries' respect.

The best-known story of his time at Brienne is the tale of the snowball fight, which became a prolonged episode in the 1920s silent movie by Abel Gance. Napoleon organised the boys into two groups and then led his troop of followers to victory over his opponents, probably with a little help from stones concealed in the snowballs. Another story tells how he confronted the wife of the school porter, who was trying to push her way into a school play without a valid ticket. When she made a fuss, he commented curtly: *Take the woman away. She is bringing licentiousness into the camp.*[1] Yet a third story recounts that he and some others were allotted small areas to make into private gardens, so he bought out the others and, having put a palisade round the space, turned it into a refuge where he could read books he liked such as a translation of Tasso's poem about the First Crusade. One 25 August, the feast of St Louis, the patron of the royal house, his garden was attacked and the palisade broken down, but Napoleon drove the enemy off with a hoe. When he wanted to be alone, he meant it.

It slowly became obvious to his teachers that Napoleon was a keen student. None of them could offer him the mathematical teaching he craved. When the inspector of schools, the Chevalier de Kéralio (1713–93), passed by in 1783, he described Napoleon as 'obedient, affable, straightforward, grateful'.[2] By then he had made two friends among the boys, one a scholarship boy like himself, the other an effeminate aristocrat, Pierre François Laugier de Bellecour. In spite or because of his altercation with the porter's wife, he was on good terms with the porter, and, though he quickly lost his own faith, he admired the simple piety of Père Charles, the curé of Brienne, who prepared him for his first Communion.

Kéralio thought that Napoleon, who would be 14 in August, would make an excellent sailor; now that England and France were at peace, there was even a chance he could have left Brienne and trained in England. His father, who was already showing signs of the cancer that was to kill him and was worried about the parlous state of the family finances, hoped Napoleon could graduate then, so that his scholarship could be passed on to Lucciano, but in the event, Napoleon was not allowed to leave Brienne for another year and the opportunity passed. By the time he graduated in summer 1784, there was another problem – Joseph.

Rochet's retrospective statue of Napoleon when he was at Brienne

Napoleon's brother had won all the academic prizes at Autun, but he did not want to be a priest. In his first extant letter, dated 25 June 1784 and addressed to his uncle, Nicolo Paravicini, Napoleon makes his own views clear. After briefly mentioning his father's visit with Napoleon's eldest sister, Elise (on their way to her school at St-Cyr), and Lucien, whom they had left behind at Brienne, he turns to the subject of his older brother. Joseph, he says, writes only two lines to their father, if he writes at all, but he writes to Napoleon himself often. Joseph is clever and has done well at school. Now instead of following his career in the church, he wants to serve the King in the army; and the very thought compels Napoleon to protest. *He has been educated for a clerical career. It is very late for him to change ...* One by one Napoleon rules out the marines, the engineers and the artillery, which leaves only the infantry *and what is a smart young infantry officer up to, three-quarters of his time, except misconducting himself.* He concludes in typically authoritarian fashion: *We shall therefore make a last effort to get him to stick to the clerical career ... or else my dear father will ... try to turn him into a lawyer.* (Joseph did in the end train as a lawyer.)[3]

Napoleon left Brienne on 17 October and reached the Ecole Royale Militaire (Royal Military School) in Paris two days later. Life in the heart of the capital was very unlike life at Brienne, in a remote part of Champagne. Napoleon found himself living in a fine Neo-Classical building designed by Louis XV's favourite architect, Gabriel (1698–1782), in a style that seemed to him only too sybaritic. To serve the 215 cadets there were, in addition to the essential teachers, a whole army of chaplains, sacristans, riding instructors, grooms, doctors, nurses, dressmakers, wigmakers, cooks, butlers and maids besides no less than 150 who were merely servants. In Paris linen was changed three times a week. Napoleon was shocked at the luxury he had to endure, possibly because he thought he saw the consequences for the morality of the students. His old friend Laugier de Bellecour had joined the institution and by now did not hide his sexual proclivities. Napoleon was disgusted and the two resorted to a brawl. Laugier complained but Napoleon was not punished and Laugier disappeared from his life. Napoleon immersed himself in his studies.

Napoleon wanted to become a gunner, an ambition that suited someone like him who excelled at the application of many branches of mathematics such as trigonometry, analytical geometry and calculus. (As an adult he would calculate logarithms for fun and test out his companions with difficult mathematical calculations.) Pierre-Simon Laplace (1749–1827), one of the most brilliant astronomers of the age and a man who could stretch him mathematically, examined him at the Ecole. France boasted a very inventive scientific community and Napoleon is said to have intervened in a demonstration of one of France's more brilliant technical feats when he cut the ropes that kept a balloonist earthbound on the nearby Champ de Mars. As at Brienne, Napoleon succeeded at mathematics and was no good at the socially graceful skills of drawing and

On St Helena Napoleon still enjoyed re-reading *The New Héloïse*. But he no longer cared for Rousseau's exaltation of human sympathy. He said that his brother Louis had been *spoilt by the reading of Jean-Jacques*.[4] As King of Holland Louis had thought about Dutch feelings instead of obeying his brother.

dancing. He was still no linguist but he had begun to read widely in modern French. He became a devotee of Rousseau.

In Napoleon's youth Jean-Jacques Rousseau had become the most popular modern author in France. He made his name with his *Discourse on the origins and foundations of inequality among men*, published in 1755. Napoleon would make notes on this essay in 1791. In the early 1760s Rousseau went on to produce three of his major works in a rush: *The New Héloïse* (1761), a story of an idealistic triangular relationship involving a husband, his young wife and the wife's tutor; *The Social Contract* (1762), a political treatise, and *Emile* (1762), a book on ideal education. All three books were censured by the authorities. Napoleon once claimed that he had first read *The New Héloïse* at the age of nine and in his 20s he probably valued it more than anything else that Rousseau wrote, but eventually, even if indirectly, he was more influenced by Rousseau's political views. Rousseau's concept of general will, which can justify overriding individual citizens' wishes in the name of all the citizens collectively, may explain Napoleon's use of referenda to get popular backing for his constitutional changes. So too the concept of civic religion may have encouraged Napoleon to see religion as social cement rather than the expression of a truth. What he certainly got from Rousseau was a youthful emphasis on the value of feeling – he shook off Rousseau as he became more cynical. Like Rousseau, who had a knack of being persecuted, Napoleon felt his own isolation acutely; but while Rousseau found relief by running away, Napoleon used his remoteness to dominate others.

On 24 February 1785, Carlo Buonaparte died – Napoleon's second extant letter is a message of consolation to his mother – putting pressure on Napoleon to speed up the completion of his studies. Family finances were already tight – Marbeuf, who had guaranteed payment for Joseph and Napoleon's education at Autun, had withdrawn his patronage and financial support – but now Napoleon felt obliged to earn some money as soon as he could. In normal circumstances an artilleryman would study the first volume of the standard textbook, the *Cours de Mathématiques* of Etienne Bézout, at the Ecole Militaire, then spend a year at artillery school, at the end of which he would be examined on the remaining three volumes. A few students, however, could short-circuit the process by completing two years' of study in one, without the need to go to artillery school, and Napoleon was allowed to do so. In Napoleon's year only 58 of those who took the examination in the whole of France passed and of these only four were from the Ecole Royale Militaire. Napoleon was placed 42nd and was the second youngest to be accepted, just behind a bitter rival, the arch royalist Le Picard de Phélipeaux (1768–99), and well before his new best friend, another royalist named Alexandre Des Mazis, who was 56th.

Napoleon had found his schooling hard. His family's finances had forced him to rush his studies and he also felt slighted both for being Corsican and for his lowly birth. He despised the idle and charming aristocrats about him who took it for granted that an agreeable, diverting life was their due. He was socially ill at ease in their company while knowing he was superior in intellect to most of them. He had made few friends and, partly because he could not believe that the men of the past whom he admired like Caesar were now in hell, he had lost the consolation of a religious faith. In one way he had been lucky. The section of the army he had chosen, the artillery, was one where technically France led the world and one in which a Frenchman could advance by skill and application.

Failed revolutionary 1785–94

Napoleon left the Ecole Militaire in October 1785 to join the La Fère regiment, which he had probably chosen because it was garrisoned in the unremarkable Provençal town of Valence, the base nearest to the coast opposite Corsica. He was just 16, had been made a second lieutenant and had no war to fight. By January 1786 he had finished his period of probation as an officer. His duties scarcely involved much effort. He had to mount guard, look after his men, attend classes. He had time to climb a mountain, go skating or write home about a pretty girl he had danced with. At only five foot six inches tall, he was below average height and, as a virgin, he must have seemed a sexual ingénu in the macho world of the army. He was short of money: his father had left the family destitute and, as he was the only son earning, he sent much of his pay home.

He had started reading more enthusiastically in his scant spare time in Paris. Now, keen to mark himself out from the crowd, he decided to try his hand at writing. Over the next few years writing became a favourite leisure occupation. According to his brother Joseph he also read widely: in translation many Latin authors, among them Caesar, and one Greek, Plutarch, who wrote parallel lives of Greek and Latin heroes; in the original French, authors of the previous century, notably the tragedians Corneille and Racine, and of the present century, especially Rousseau; and in translation too the bogus epic of *Ossian*, concocted by a Scottish fraudster named James Macpherson (1736–96).

Napoleon was restless. He started to adopt patterns of behaviour that he followed for several years. He sought permission to go to Corsica as much as possible, partly to help his family, partly because he could matter in Corsica, and partly because he believed in Corsica. He made sure he was up-to-date both with military ideas and with political developments. Whenever he experienced any problems with his immediate superiors, he would appeal to a more senior figure, even if that meant travelling to Paris. It took him years to be noticed as a soldier, but long before that he had already begun to master the art of manipulating those who mattered.

Napoleon cared about the fate of Corsica, for there he could attain the things closest to his heart: power and glory. He first went to Corsica in September 1786 and, on the dubious grounds of suffering from 'an ague', got permission to stay there until December 1787. Back in Paris that winter he picked up a prostitute in the notorious area of the Palais Royal, home of the royal dukes of Orleans, and had sex for the first time. In January 1788 he was back in Corsica and did not return to his regiment, now in Auxonne in Burgundy, till late May. In peaceful times such absenteeism was overlooked, especially as his private studies were going well. He impressed Lombard, his mathematics teacher, who recommended him to the senior commander in town, Baron du Teil, whose brother was author of one of the best textbooks on the use of modern artillery.

Jean Baptiste de Gribeauval (1715–89) had modernised the French artillery, after his ideas had received the backing of King Louis XVI on his accession to the throne in 1774, giving the French guns that were lighter, faster and more accurate than their predecessors. Four years later the Chevalier Jean du Teil (1733–1820), produced a textbook on how the new guns should be used, recommending the concentration of overwhelming force at critical moments in a battle. Napoleon studied the writings of other modern French theorists as well. From Jacques Antoine Hippolyte, Comte de Guibert (1743–90) he learned that armies should aim to move rapidly and live off the land wherever they found themselves. From Pierre de Bourcet's *Principes des guerres de montagne* ('Principles of mountain warfare', 1764–71) he learned that divisions should be separated in order to move rapidly and come together to win a battle. In the library at Auxonne Napoleon was also able to read about the exploits of famous generals in the distant past, like Cyrus the Great of Persia, Alexander the Great and Julius Caesar, and the recent past, like Louis XIV's ablest general Turenne, the Austrian Prince Eugène, who had defeated Louis XIV's armies in Italy, Louis XV's ablest general the Marshal de Saxe and above all the nemesis of Louis XV's armies in central Europe, Napoleon's favourite, Frederick the Great, King of Prussia (reigned 1740–86), who was himself a clear and perceptive writer on military affairs. The art of drill and manoeuvre that had been prized in the 18th century had been elegant, lifesaving and cautious. Napoleon's style of fighting would be dramatic, bloody and decisive, but as yet he had no chance to try it out.

In France, however, things were changing. The problems began with the state's dire finances. Louis XVI knew that there was no adequate system for raising the funds that the state required. Taxation was still based on the perverse principle that the poor paid proportionately more than the rich – indeed the rich could sometimes avoid tax altogether. Louis XVI sought help from one adviser after another, tried calling an assembly of the nobles, and exiled and then recalled the Parlement of Paris, until in the end he agreed to a meeting of the Estates General for May 1789. Under pressure from the third estate (all those who were neither clergy nor the nobility and in practice mostly lawyers), the division of the 'estates' quickly broke down and a national, one-chamber assembly was formed.

When the assembly failed to produce the required consensus, the situation worsened. Louis XVI was suspected of wishing to use force to re-establish control, so on 14 July 1789 a Paris mob stormed the city arsenal known as the Bastille, lynched its governor and seized the arms stored there. Louis did nothing. All over the countryside peasants destroyed manor records that listed their ancient obligations to their lords; sometimes they strung up the lords and burnt their houses. Still Louis did not react. In August the Assembly abolished the ancient obligations and in October the King was forced to leave Versailles and take up permanent residence in the centre of Paris in the Tuileries Palace. He was no longer an absolute monarch. With little forethought the king had been replaced with a weak executive – the National Assembly – that had no means either of paying off debts or of raising money to fight a war.

Napoleon first encountered the unrest that was sweeping across France when his regiment was sent to a neighbouring town called Seurre, where its presence seems to have been enough to keep the population quiet. Napoleon, however, was anxious for action. Once again he got permission to go home to Corsica. When he arrived there, late in September 1789, he found the island in a state of political agitation. Among the new politicians who had emerged was Antoine Christophe Saliceti (1757–1809), chosen to represent the third estate in the Estates General. Early in 1790 Saliceti persuaded his fellow citizens in the National Assembly (by now also called the Constituent Assembly), which had just incorporated the island into France, to tell Paoli that he could come back. Paoli, still hoping for some measure of independence for Corsica, returned to the island that year and was made a lieutenant-general.

Napoleon managed to stay in Corsica throughout 1790 – when he tried to sail to the mainland rough weather prevented him – and it was there and then that he became a professional politician. Unlike

A portrait of Napoleon as a general of the Army of the Interior

many more privileged aristocrats in France, he had so little status on the mainland that he had little to lose if the political system changed radically. In Corsica, however, where his family counted, he could use family connections to become prominent as a conservative or as a radical. He found that among his fellow townsmen in Ajaccio the radicals were dominant. An obvious way of advancing the Bonaparte family, then, was to lead them. In a 1787 essay on

'Love of Glory and Love of Country', he had praised a Corsican patriot who would rather die than live dishonourably. Now that he had the chance to act nobly on his native island, he was more pragmatic. He got his brother Joseph elected to the town council of Ajaccio, hounded out any conservatives who opposed him, and became a founder member of Ajaccio's Jacobin Club, modelled on the leading revolutionary organisation in Paris. The commander of the garrison grumbled about him to the Ministry of War, pointing out that Napoleon and his family had received a lot of help from official sources and now he was intent on causing trouble.

Between August 1789 and September 1791 the National Assembly, renamed the Constituent Assembly, was preoccupied with constitution-making. The Declaration of the Rights of Man and the Citizen drew out what was implied by the assertion that all men are free and equal in rights. Citizens have an inalienable right to property. They are to be free from arbitrary arrest and imprisonment, free to have opinions, even in religion, and free from taxation without consent. Not all Frenchmen were equal, however. All adult males were indeed citizens but only those with property of a certain value could vote; and they had to have still more property to be voted for.

France's administration was reorganised. Everything must be uniform. France was divided into 83 departments, which took their names from rivers or mountains, the departments were sub-divided into districts and districts subdivided into communes. At the same time the mass of different courts was abolished. Still more radically, administrators and judges were to be elected, not appointed, and their posts could not be bought.

Soldiers and sailors too from now on, at least in principle, would become officers by merit, not by social position. In fact it was impossible to institute such a system straight away, but the idea of a citizens' army and a citizens' navy had been mooted and was not forgotten.

When Napoleon returned to the mainland in January 1791, his politics did not go down well with his royalist fellow officers in Auxonne. He was tactfully promoted to the rank of first lieutenant and sent to Valence to join the 4th or Grenoble Regiment. Four days later Louis XVI, along with his wife, Marie Antoinette, and their children, was stopped at Varennes attempting to escape to Austria; for this reason all officers were ordered to take an oath of loyalty to the National Assembly and the constitution that would dissolve it. So many royalist officers resigned that revolutionaries began to find that they got the chance of quick promotion. (In the navy this proved disastrous, as most officers were royalist nobles.) Napoleon took the new oath without a qualm and, though careful to drink His Majesty's health when it proved politic, was also quick to join the Jacobin Club of Valence. But his eye was on his island. Yet again he asked for leave.

Napoleon got permission from General du Teil, who was superior to his commanding officer, to go back to Corsica on the grounds that his uncle was dying. His uncle dutifully died, leaving Napoleon and Joseph at last well off. He and Joseph bought a house in Ajaccio, where Joseph already headed the Directory that ran affairs in that town. Meanwhile, though Paoli and his followers seemed to have become all-powerful, they began to quarrel among themselves. Napoleon then heard that all soldiers must rejoin their regiments. To continue to wield influence in Corsica, he must find a reason to stay.

Napoleon found it by dint of artful electioneering. He meant to be one of the two lieutenant-colonels of Corsican volunteers known as National Guardsmen. Uncle Lucien's funds bribed many of the voters. Then, on the night of the election, 31 March 1792, his men kidnapped one of the three commissioners who were to supervise the election from a house belonging to Pozzo di Borgo (1764–1842), his chief rival and a supporter of Paoli. When, on the day of the election itself, di Borgo tried to speak in public, he was almost knifed before being hurried off the platform. The volunteer soldiers saw sense (in a Napoleonic definition of that word) and Napoleon was chosen.

Napoleon and his fellow revolutionaries attempted to consolidate their grip on the island. In order to complete the rout of all royalists, the revolutionaries decided to make an example of a group of priests who refused to take an oath of loyalty to the new Civic Constitution of the Church. Saliceti went on to insinuate that the piety of many Paolistas showed that they were covert royalists. Napoleon tried to seize Ajaccio's citadel, but could not eject the royalist governor, who threatened to turn his cannon on the city. Napoleon had to give way, but he had shown that he was loyal to the increasingly radical line being taken in Paris, even if he could not force his compatriots to endorse it. He also, however, had a lot of explaining to do. He had been absent without leave for so long that officially he had lost his job with his regiment. By the summer of 1792, it was imperative that he return to Paris to save himself.

As in Provence, however, Napoleon was able to politic his way out of trouble, lobbying in Paris for support so successfully that he was forgiven, made a captain, and given back pay. Though told to return to his regiment, he stayed on in Paris, waiting for his reinstatement to be ratified by the Minister of War.

The mood of Paris alarmed him. Early in 1792, when the new Legislative Assembly (which had replaced the Constituent Assembly in October 1791) had begun sitting, the lawyers who dominated it – the liberal nobles and clerics of the National Assembly had already disappeared from political life – had taken on an enemy much more formidable than the Pope. Austria had attempted to speak up for King Louis; now Austria must be checked. In April 1792 the King found himself obliged to declare war on his brother-in-law. As the armies of Austria, a traditional enemy and the homeland of their hated queen, threatened France,

An engraving of Napoleon as First Consul of the French Republic

a patriotic and hysterical mood seized the capital. On 10 August the mob reacted savagely. While Louis hesitated, as he was loathe to shed blood, people with no such inhibitions rushed the Swiss Guards who were meant to protect him, massacred them and seized the royal family.

Napoleon witnessed this turbulent event at first hand. He hurried to the Carrousel near the Tuileries Palace and watched the horror from the window of an apartment belonging to a former comrade from Brienne. Venturing out onto the streets, he met a group of men carrying a head at the end of a pike. *Seeing me fairly well dressed and looking like a gentleman, they came up to me to make me cry* Long live the nation! *which I did without making any difficulty, as you can imagine ... When the palace had been forced and the King taken to the heart of the Assembly ... I dared to go into the {Tuileries} gardens. Never, since, has any of my battles given me an idea of so many corpses as I got from seeing all the Swiss ... I saw women of some respectability committing the worst indecencies on the bodies of the Swiss.* It was an experience that still haunted him on St Helena.[5]

By mid-October 1792 he was back in Corsica for what became his final venture on home territory. Though he had moved against some clerical Paolistas earlier in the year, Napoleon still recognised that Paoli's popularity on the island made him the key to political power there. In May 1792 he had written to Joseph from Paris: *Keep on close terms with General Paoli. He is everything, and can do everything. He will be all-important in a future that no one in the world can predict.*[6] He had done all he could to stay on his native island as long as he could and he had seen his family recover a position of importance there. (He had thought of writing a history of Corsica.) Now he would make a final attempt to gain outright control of Ajaccio and ensure that Corsica would be a modern island, which espoused his own 'Jacobin' views.

He was to be cruelly disillusioned. In recent elections, while Napoleon was absent, Pozzo di Borgo had ousted Joseph. When he spoke with Paoli in late 1792, Napoleon found that their political views had diverged: though Paoli still wanted some measure of independence for Corsica, he was no radical, and was horrified by the prospect that the King might be executed.

While Ajaccio, where Napoleon spent most of his time from Christmas 1792 to February 1793, was somnolent, Paris was tense. France's new armies had first routed the Prussians (in September 1792) before defeating the Austrians (in November 1792). On 21 January 1793 Louis XVI was executed. In the Edict of Fraternity, issued in November 1792, France had stated that it would attack any despotic regime anywhere in Europe. In February and March 1793 it made good its word by declaring war on the kingdoms of Spain and Britain, whose Prime Minister, Pitt, became Napoleon's chief enemy.

Napoleon was to have a role only in the least important of any prospective campaign, the venture to attack the island of Sardinia, which had allied itself with Britain and whose downfall would have put pressure on Italian states like Florence. It turned out to be a humiliating experience. Napoleon was called in to act as number three in an amphibious expedition launched from Corsica against La Maddelena, an islet just off the north coast of Sardinia. The attack failed and Napoleon had to retreat. Back in Corsica he found himself unpopular, stigmatised by some sailors as an aristocrat, and he was almost lynched. In a second interview, Paoli expressed his disgust at the execution of the King and, when Napoleon maintained that it was Louis XVI's own fault, Paoli left the room in a rage. The two men never spoke again.

On St Helena Napoleon explained what he thought distinguished the two leading British politicians of the day, the younger William Pitt and his Francophile opponent Charles James Fox (1751–1806). *In Fox the heart extinguished genius, whereas in Pitt genius dried up the heart.*[7]

Soon afterwards the increasingly radical Saliceti began to plot to be rid of Paoli. At the Jacobin Club in Toulon, Napoleon's brother Lucien, the orator of the family, denounced Paoli as a traitor. From Paris the new assembly, the Convention, which had replaced the Legislative Assembly in September 1792, summoned Paoli to answer the charges in person. He pleaded old age and defied the government to act. With no troops available from the mainland to back them up, the plans of Saliceti and Napoleon came to nothing. In the end it was they who lost out. Paolistas sacked the Bonapartes' house in Ajaccio and gutted their farms.

Napoleon joined Joseph and Saliceti in Bastia, in the north of the island, while Letizia and her daughters hid until Napoleon managed to find them. They all embarked for Toulon and arrived on the mainland virtually penniless. The Bonapartes would never return to Corsica.

Napoleon's prolonged attempt to count as a political force in Corsica had ended in failure. Only in one sense was he vindicated. Though Napoleon had begun as a Corsican patriot, sympathetic to independence, his Jacobinism had led him to favour a centralised France. Now Paoli found that it was impossible to win independence for Corsica. He had to opt for French or British rule. He chose Britain. In June 1794 the Council of Corsica offered the Crown to King George III, who accepted it. Soon the British forced the difficult Paoli to retire to England. Pozzo di Borgo was governor until in 1796 the French quietly recaptured the island. Of the English Paoli said, 'sono mercanti' ('they are traders'). It was a phrase Napoleon remembered when he called the English a nation of shopkeepers.

Circumstances had forced Napoleon and his family to commit themselves to France. Luckily for them all his commitment was to be whole-hearted; and, having been beaten on a tiny stage, he would triumph on a huge one. It was only by coming to France as a refugee that Napoleon was able to have a career that could match his dreams. It was only as a Frenchmen that his gifts for political manoeuvring could make him famous and it was only as a French soldier that he could show the world that he was a military genius.

As so often, events in Paris dictated the shape of the world in which he would operate. Since the middle of 1792 Parisian politics had been dominated by the struggle between a more moderate faction – often known as the Girondins – and the more radical Jacobins, whom Napoleon supported, under the ideologue Maximilien Robespierre. In June 1793, the Girondins, who had

Napoleon views the siege of Toulon from the ramparts

argued against the execution of the King, were purged from the Convention.

Robespierre and the Jacobins believed in the one indivisible republic. Now, as they consolidated their grip on power in Paris, protests in the provinces turned into open revolt. In Toulon, where the Bonapartes were living, anti-Jacobins began to try to wrest power from the ruling factions, closing the Jacobin club and sentencing leading Jacobins to death. What was worse, once Toulon had ejected its Jacobins, it called in the British navy under Admiral Lord Hood (1727–1816), the man who would take over Corsica next year. For the second time, the family was forced to

leave home because of their political allegiances. Lucien Bonaparte and his dependants had to flee. Napoleon rejoined his regiment, the 4th Artillery, now stationed in Nice. Saliceti saved the family from destitution, telling the Convention in Paris that the Bonapartes had sacrificed everything for the Republic. The Convention voted them compensation of 600,000 francs. In spite of this show of support, Saliceti persuaded Napoleon that it would be worthwhile to go further to prove himself a sound Jacobin. For some years Napoleon had dabbled in writing. Now he wrote a pamphlet that attracted some notice, *Le Souper de Beaucaire* ('Supper at Beaucaire').

Le Souper de Beaucaire is a dialogue about current politics between an army officer, a businessman from Marseille, a man from Montpellier and a manufacturer from Nîmes and a moderate republican. The soldier, a veiled version of Napoleon himself, does most of the talking (like 'Socrates' in Plato's dialogues). Against the background of the federalist revolts against the centralising Jacobins then breaking out all over France, the soldier persuades the others to back the authority of Paris against these counter-revolutionaries. After he has elaborated his arguments the civilians are convinced and the businessman shares a bottle of champagne with everyone. Napoleon's pamphlet was brought to the attention of Augustin Robespierre (1763–94), brother of Maximilien, and Napoleon duly became a Robespierrist protégé. So long as Robespierre and the Jacobins clung to power, Napoleon was safe.

The surrender of Toulon to the British gave Napoleon his first real opportunity to demonstrate his military skill. As the Convention set about retaking Toulon from the British, Saliceti was able to ensure that Napoleon, now a major, would be in charge of the artillery in the proposed attack. Napoleon quickly lost patience with the cautious generals he was supposed to serve under. As Saliceti's protégé, he was able to pull strings to get rid of one; the next, a dentist who could not stand the sight of blood, quickly resigned and was replaced by General Dugommier (1738–94), who was willing to let Napoleon do what he wanted. After his humiliating defeat as the number three in the attack on La Maddelena, he finally had command.

Napoleon had noticed that the harbour of Toulon, like the harbour of Ajaccio, was dominated by a headland at its entrance. If he could control this headland, called L'Eguilette, the little needle, he would command the harbour. The headland was heavily defended but on the night of 17/18 December Napoleon led his troops up to the fort on the headland and, after two hours' intense hand-to-hand fighting, in which Napoleon was wounded in the leg, took it. This enabled him to place his guns where they would threaten Hood's forces and so force the English fleet out of the harbour. Napoleon was now a figure of consequence, profiting from his Robespierrist connections. He was made brigadier-general and given command of the artillery of the so-called Army of Italy, a ragbag of a force meant to conquer Piedmont and so open the route to the Austrian lands of northern Italy.

Before Napoleon could make his mark on Italy, he had to survive one political crisis after another. First, in August 1794, the brothers Robespierre were toppled from power and guillotined. After nine months of Terror, in which around 16,000 people, many of them in the rebellious provinces, had been guillotined, the architects of the repression themselves became its last victims. As their protégé Napoleon became vulnerable and Saliceti, anxious to protect himself from the charge of being a Jacobin, denounced Napoleon. Soon he and Lucien were imprisoned, Napoleon guilty, it seemed, of a mysterious visit to the enemy state of Genoa. While Lucien, the eloquent orator, pleaded for forgiveness, Napoleon, electing to be cool, read about earlier campaigns in Italy, from Hannibal onwards, making notes on the Italian campaign of the French general Marshal Maillebois in 1745. When questioned about his loyalties, he cited his services to the republic at Toulon and waited patiently.

When Maximilian Robespierre (1758–94) fell, Napoleon had to explain why he had changed his mind about the man whom he had admired. *I loved* him, he said, *and believed in* him. *But, if he were my father, I myself would have stabbed him to death if he aspired to tyranny.* [8]

After Napoleon had spent ten days in prison, Saliceti, conscious perhaps that Napoleon had shed his Jacobin beliefs, suddenly said there was no charge to answer and Napoleon was freed.

General Bonaparte 1795–9

The men who brought Robespierre down were no crusaders for a great cause. They were just worried that they might be the next to die. Like Robespierre they had probably voted for the execution of Louis XVI, like him they accepted the constitutional changes made in 1789–91, like him they had become committed to a continuing external war against France's neighbours, and like him they wished to crush internal dissent. While Robespierre had tried to keep prices down for the sake of the poor, they knew that they wanted a republic controlled by people like themselves who had an eye for a quick profit. The electors must be well off, the elected still better off and no one person should be too powerful.

After forgetting Augustin Robespierre with a half-hearted sigh and shedding his Jacobin beliefs, Napoleon began to make his way towards the top of this new, corrupt world. Gone were the austere practical clothes that had been a sign of correct thinking. Women were now so determined to dress like ancient Greeks that they took to wearing flimsy diaphanous robes and decking out their bodies with jewels, while wealthy young men flaunted their attractions with outlandish costumes and ran up enormous tailors' bills. Napoleon, instinctively puritanical and yet easily dazzled by a sophisticated set, went to parties. Lacking social graces, he seems to have had little luck with women, at least at first; he was more an observer than a participant in the *louche* goings-on. After meeting an 'It-girl' of the time, he wrote: *This city is always the same. Everything for pleasure, everything for women, everything for spectacles, for balls, for walks, for artists' studios.* [9] The economy remained unstable, government finances shaky and the poor wretched, but bankers, army contractors and property speculators prospered. Only two things worried the new ruling class: defeat in war abroad and rebellion at home. They needed men who reassured them.

After he had been restored to favour, Napoleon returned to his overriding concern of the past few years: how to retake Corsica from the British. But though he could drive an English fleet from the harbour of Toulon – the young General Lazare Hoche (1768–97), soon to emerge as Napoleon's rival, had had a similar success against an English-sponsored invasion in southern Brittany – defeating the English on the open sea was virtually impossible. The English already had naval superiority off both the Mediterranean and the Atlantic coasts of France and could be defeated only if they came on land. Corsica would have to wait.

Napoleon had been called to Paris and told to provide the artillery arm of the force that would bring order to the rebellious departments of Brittany. But to do so would have meant a demotion and serving under Hoche, so Napoleon, perhaps also wary of getting involved in civil war, refused to obey his orders. Having done so much research into a possible Italian campaign, he asked that he be posted instead to the Army of Italy, but the Minister of War refused. Even when this minister was replaced, Napoleon was offered only a desk job planning possible future campaigns. He was so desperate for action that he even thought of going to Turkey to fight for the Sultan. In September he was told that his

In his lifetime Lazare Hoche, *brave, intelligent and talented*, had been a rival to Napoleon in love, politics and war, but as he had died young, in 1797, Napoleon could afford to be generous. Hoche, he said on St Helena, *was a wonderful man, very clever and impressive in appearance.* [10]

disobedience had cost him his rank of general. A month later, in October 1795, a crisis in Paris changed his life.

The new constitution that would set up the Directory (government by a committee of five 'Directors') had been approved by a plebiscite, but one provision remained unpopular. The members of the existing Convention had decided that two-thirds of the new lower house, the Council of 500, should be drawn from their own members. The mood of Paris became restive. Nervously the Convention placed the able Paul François Jean Nicolas Barras (1755–1829), a former viscount, in charge of the Army of the Interior, though Barras had little military experience. Barras knew that if there were to be trouble, he would need the help of a gunner with experience and a ruthless temperament. When an insurrection began, Barras, who knew Napoleon from Toulon, begged him for help. Napoleon asked where the guns were and was told that they were six miles away at Sablons and a royalist-led mob was already on its way to capture them. Napoleon called for Murat (1767–1815), a cavalry officer whose only method of fighting was to charge, and told him to reach Sablons first with 200 men. Murat arrived just in time and saved Napoleon 40 guns, with which to defend the Tuileries Palace, where the Convention met. Heavily outnumbered, but far better armed, Napoleon disposed his troops in such a way that the rebels were obliged to execute a frontal attack in the narrow streets that led to the Tuileries. A few lethal rounds of 'grape-shot' (or, more accurately, canister shot) – small balls that scattered when fired from cannon – and the struggle was settled. Hundreds died.

Over and over again since the attack on the Bastille in July 1789, determined Parisian mobs had defeated trained soldiers. This time, with only 'a whiff of grape-shot' (Thomas Carlyle's phrase), Napoleon had dispersed an armed crowd. Grateful politicians, relieved that their Republic had been saved, cheered him. Three weeks later, on 27 October 1795 (5 Brumaire in the new

'The whiff of grape-shot'. Napoleon gives the order to fire the cannon upon the insurgents on the steps of Saint-Roch

revolutionary calendar) the constitution was inaugurated. Barras became one of the Directors and Napoleon was granted the rank of full General.

Hitherto Napoleon's chief correspondent had been his brother Joseph. Napoleon wrote to give his brother a brief account of his fighting on the streets of Paris: *The enemy attacked us at the Tuileries. We killed a large number of them ... As usual I haven't had a scratch.*[11] Two months later he had a new correspondent and was writing: *I awake filled with you. Your image, and the intoxicating pleasures of last night, allow my senses no rest.*[12] The terse rhythm of the sentences and the spare diction have been transformed, for Napoleon had fallen in love.

It was some years since he had lost his virginity to the prostitute he met near the Palais Royal; and there had been women when he wanted them. He had given Louis a copy of the favourite romance of the time, *Paul et Virginie*, and Napoleon had tried his

hand at a love story of his own. *Clisson et Eugénie*, his brief, unpub-
lished attempt at a version of *The New Héloïse*, was based on his
own flirtation with Bernardine Eugénie Désirée (1777–1860),
the younger sister of his brother Joseph's wife, Julie Clary (1771–
1845). Its hero, Clisson, is a young man devoted to warfare who
has had a spectacular career that has made him many enemies. In
a mood of self-pity he retreats into himself, until he is rescued by
the attention of two young girls. He falls in love with the younger
one, eventually marries her, has children by her and is happy. At
the end he must return to fighting and, having written one last
letter to Eugénie about his undying love, rushes into the centre of
a fight and is killed by a thousand blows. In actual life Napoleon's
romantic effusions were little more than posturing. As he had no
wish to go down south to see his Eugénie, he contented himself
with writing her letters.

This new romance was quite different. In the summer of 1795
Napoleon met the mistress of Barras, his chief political ally. Rose de
Beauharnais (1763–1814), born Rose Tachscher de la Pagerie, was
an exotic creature, the first of three sisters born on the Caribbean
island of Martinique. She had come to Paris to marry the Vicomte
de Beauharnais and dutifully produced a son, Eugène (1781–
1824), and a daughter, Hortense (1783–1837), before falling
out of love with her capricious and unfaithful husband. They had
divorced in 1785, but nevertheless, towards the end of the Terror,
which had already claimed her ex-husband's life, she found herself
awaiting execution. In prison she had shared her cell with Lazare
Hoche, before cheating death when Robespierre was killed before
she could be. She was penniless, a widow with two children, and
she made men feel protective. With her uninhibited sense of style
she became one of the leaders of fashionable society. She attached
herself to Barras because it paid. She had no strong feelings about
much beyond clothes, so she was taken aback when Barras's young
protégé revealed a sexual passion for her (and a desire to possess

Joséphine Beauharnais in a sketch by Isabey

her exclusively) that overwhelmed him. She consented to be his lover – Barras seems to have been relieved to have her taken off his hands – but may have been surprised when he asked her to be his wife. There was a foretaste of his need to dominate her in his demand that she should change her name to Joséphine; and both pretended they were rich (which was true of neither of them) and falsified their ages (she gave her age as 28, as the only birth certificate she could find was her younger sister's, and he as 27, as the only birth certificate he could find was Joseph's).

The two were married in a civil ceremony in March 1796 (the windy month of Ventôse). The real gap in their ages was six years (Napoleon was 26, Joséphine was 32), but facts worried neither party if the facts were inconvenient. What may have concerned her more was the prospect of living with a man of volcanic emotions. These feelings became evident once they were parted: *I have not passed a day without loving you*, he wrote. *If I separate myself from you with the speed of the Rhône in full spate, it is so as to see you more quickly … The day when you say, I love you less, will be the last day of my love or the day of my death … Living for Joséphine is the story of my life … You must be here beside me, on my heart, in my arms, on my mouth … Without ceasing I repeatedly remember all we have done, your kisses, your tears, your loveable jealousy … Far from you, nights are long, boring and sad, near you, I regret it's not already night … A thousand kisses all over you …*[13]

If she had to receive such letters, they would be more amusing if the author was far away. There is at any rate no sign that she regretted the rapid disappearance of her new husband from her social scene; and when he asked her to follow him, she found endless excuses for delay. He, as always, was in a rush. Barras had recommended him to Lazare Carnot (1753–1823), the man responsible for the organisation of the army, and Carnot agreed to give Napoleon command of the Army of Italy. The honeymoon lasted two days and two nights and then Napoleon was off.

The Italian campaign of 1796–7 made and has preserved Napoleon's reputation as one of the greatest of all generals. His battles have been studied at military academies like West Point and Sandhurst; and though some critics have pointed out flaws in Napoleon's style of fighting – one has maintained that he blundered to win his victories – there is no doubt that at the time his style seemed novel, bewildering and decisive. If he put himself between his enemy and the enemy's base, the old (and old-fashioned) generals he fought did not see that he had given them an equivalent opportunity, as they were placed between Napoleon and his base. He knew the ground he fought over from maps, he was not fighting on home territory and he could misjudge the effect of climate and terrain on his troops. As he seemed to be inexhaustible, he often forgot that his soldiers were not. If he paused, he did so only from necessity. He did not wait for orders from Paris; indeed, the more confident he became, the less he bothered to consult anyone. In the end he went on to arrange the terms of treaties and then sign them, anticipating correctly that the government would not dare to criticise him for acting independently. It is hard to point out to a successful general that he has been incorrect.

Though Napoleon had been successful at Toulon and on the streets of Paris, those were relatively minor victories, in which he had not had outright command. Now he was faced with leading a major campaign. At first his officers regarded him as a political general, a man who owed his job to his connections. That judgement was sound, but they did not realise that Napoleon had spent months working out what needed to be done. His chief of staff Louis Alexandre Berthier (1753–1815) was in his 40s, and of the other generals Jean Sérurier (1742–1819) was in his 50s, Pierre-François Charles Augereau (1757–1816) and André Massena (1758–1817) both 38. Whatever they felt about their 26-year-old leader when they first met him, he immediately impressed them with his logic, clarity and presence. By convincing them that his plans were feasible, he had won them over for many years. He then had to convince the men.

Years later, in exile on St Helena he had the time to work out what he should have said to them at the start of the campaign: *Soldiers, you are naked, badly fed. People owe us a lot, but they cannot give us anything. Your patience and the courage you show in the midst of these mountains are wonderful, but they do not gain you any glory. I am leading you into the most fertile plains in the world. Rich provinces, large cities will be in our power, and there you will have riches, honour and glory. Soldiers, would you fail to be courageous!*[14] In reality, Napoleon's soldiers would have to wait before he led them into the most fertile plains in the world.

For centuries, Italy had been a land of city-states. By the late 18th century a few republics remained, such as Genoa and Venice, both now mere shadows of their former selves, while monarchs with connections outside the peninsula controlled the most powerful cities. In the south, Naples together with Sicily formed a united kingdom ruled by the family of Bourbon-Parma, whose senior member was the King of Spain. The Pope ruled Rome and a swathe of land spanning central Italy. In the northwest the kingdom of Sardinia straddled the Alps with Savoy on the French side and Piedmont and its capital Turin on the Italian side. But the chief external influence on northern Italy, and France's main foe, was Austria. From Vienna the Holy Roman Emperor ruled the Tyrol in the northeast and Lombardy (centred on Milan) and his younger brother was Grand Duke of Tuscany, whose capital was Florence. Several tiny duchies like Modena and Parma, whose rulers struggled to survive, further complicated the political map.

The Austrians had been at war with France since 1792 and they could rely on the support of the King of Sardinia, whose troops would be in the front line. Napoleon's plan was to separate the Sardinian-Piedmontese forces from their Austrian allies, eliminate the Sardinian-Piedmontese first, then turn on the Austrians. That involved forgetting about the rich plains and heading off instead into the hilly, often mountainous lands of northwest Italy. Within days he had destroyed any appearance of allied cohesion. Though he had fewer men (some 37,000 to his enemies' 57,000), Napoleon's armies, under his sole command, were more cohesive. In late April a few battles in quick succession first isolated the Piedmontese by driving a wedge between them and the Austrians, then, while one force held off the Austrians, the main force veered towards the Piedmontese capital of Turin and persuaded the King to sue for an armistice. By the end of the month, having concluded the armistice at Cherasco, the Piedmontese had been eliminated and Napoleon could concentrate on the more serious foe.

Austria had the resources as well as the liabilities of an ancient imperial power. The Holy Roman Empire was based in Austria but included Bohemia and the many semi-independent states of Germany, such as Bavaria, Baden, Hanover, Saxony and the most powerful, Brandenburg-Prussia. It was a loose collection of states bound together by a nominal allegiance to the Emperor; some of the states, such as Brandenburg, which was the possession of the King of Prussia, and Hanover, the possession of the King of England, had links outside the Empire and some, such as Bavaria, were even allies of France. Traditionally the Holy Roman Emperor was the head of the Habsburg family. The latest in that line, Emperor Francis II (1768–1835), was young, but the Empire of which he was the head, a medieval institution that went back nearly a thousand years, was old; and old men ran it. They were ill prepared for Napoleon's rapid and ferocious style of fighting.

Having conquered in the hills, Napoleon made for the plains of Lombardy. In order to reach them he had to cross to the northern bank of the River Po. He was able to effect his plans by manoeuvring behind a screen of cavalry and, though he failed to trap the main Austrian army under the 72-year-old General Beaulieu, his personal daring while his men captured the bridge at Lodi on 10 May – he positioned himself close to the bridge, within range of Austrian guns, in order to have the best placement for his guns – earned him their admiration. He ordered a frontal attack by the bridge while sending his cavalry to find a ford, in the hope that they could attack the Austrians from behind (luckily, they found one). At another point on the Po, Piacenza, his troops astonished the Austrians by crossing the 400-metre-wide river on boats while under direct fire from the opposite bank. On 15 May, he had his reward: he entered Milan as a hero.

All this had been achieved, Napoleon believed, because he alone was in charge. When he received notice from Paris that the army was to be split into two, between François Christophe Kellerman (1735–1820) in the north and himself in the south, he protested and the Directors backed down. They then tried to insist that, instead of moving north against the Austrians in the Tyrol, he should concentrate on causing the Papal tiara to totter. Napoleon, who saw that the Austrians were the real threat, was shrewder than his masters. In Milan, he was keen to appear to favour the liberal middle classes by advocating the creation of a republic, while forcing the ruling nobles to disgorge huge sums of money and their most precious works of art for transport back to Paris and imposing heavy taxes on the Milanese to pay his soldiers' back pay. He also persisted in concentrating his forces in the north. He moved away from Milan, which promptly revolted, but a little savagery in the city of Pavia, where he had thought to kill the entire garrison but opted instead for unbridled looting, soon brought a delegation from Milan to sue for peace. His one failure, one that irked him, occurred in his domestic life: he was still unable to persuade Joséphine to join him.

Joséphine did not even appreciate his literary skill, for she left many of his letters unopened. She much preferred the physical attentions of Hippolyte Charles (1772–1837), a smart, gallant little hussar, who was funny, dishonest, extravagant and a lingering lover. Napoleon became desperate and threatened the Directors that if she did not join him, he would return to Paris to fetch her. Eventually Joséphine and her pug, who had bitten her husband when they first made love, were bundled into a carriage, along with Napoleon's brother Joseph, the future general Andoche Junot (1771–1813) – and Hippolyte Charles. On the way south Joseph busied himself writing a romantic novel, while Joséphine flirted with Junot to gain his sympathy and contrived to sleep, whenever they stopped, in the same bedroom as Charles. Once they arrived, Napoleon spent 48 hours in Joséphine's arms before turning his thoughts to Mantua, an Austrian-controlled city commanding the passes to the Alps in the north and the routes west to Milan and east to Venice. At the time he seems to have known no reason why he should get rid of Charles.

In June 1796, to show his loyalty to the Directory's official anticlericalism, he did eventually make a brief excursion south into papal territory in Bologna, just enough to make the Pope disgorge some of the most famous works of art in the world, before agreeing to an armistice, which was eventually signed in February 1797. All the time Napoleon was assuring his government of his contempt for the priesthood and reassuring the cardinal he negotiated with of his reverence for the Holy Father. While this was going on, he also made a shrewd military move by taking the Tuscan port of Leghorn so as to deny it to the British. By late June 1796 the Austrians had a new commander, Count Dagobert Sigismond von Wurmser, who in his mid-70s was even older than Beaulieu.

The second part of the Italian campaign involved a series of elaborate manoeuvres to neutralise Mantua's importance. Despite previous defeats the Austrians managed to get to Mantua first and reinforced its garrison to number 20,000 men, whom the city could not feed for long. Meanwhile two other Austrian armies, with over 40,000 men between them, descended by the Brenner Pass through the Dolomites into the Austrian Tyrol. Napoleon had been in Verona but had to abandon it for fear of being overwhelmed by superior numbers. It took him three days of hard fighting, much of it on marshy ground, to protect Verona from a two-pronged Austrian attack. As at Lodi, he won a spectacular battle at a river crossing, this time at Arcola on the Adige, to the

A detail from the portrait of Napoleon on the bridge at Arcola by Jean-Antoine Gros

south of Verona; and his own charge across the bridge became a legendary achievement, celebrated on paper by himself and on canvas by an artist named Jean-Antoine Gros (1771–1835) whom Joséphine found in Genoa. In the end he managed to prevent the two prongs from joining forces and made both armies retreat.

In Genoa Joséphine found personal solace with her delightful

Charles. When Napoleon returned to his base in Milan, he was devastated to find that she was not there. By the time she did return, however, and tried to placate him by hosting a ball, more urgent political considerations had forced themselves upon him. His former boss Saliceti had come to Italy too, intent on looting as much as he could and, when Napoleon protested, intent on destroying Napoleon's reputation at home. The Directors sent an envoy, Henri Clarke (1765–1818), to report on Napoleon. Fortunately Clarke came to the conclusion that Napoleon was a man of genius and Saliceti a rogue. The Directors authorised Napoleon to act as he thought fit. At last, just as the Austrians were about to launch a force of 70,000 into Italy to relieve their garrison in Mantua, the Directors sent Napoleon the reinforcements he had been requesting for some time. Napoleon, as usual, acted first. One final victory at Rivoli sent the Austrian army into retreat, old General Wurmser had to surrender and by spring of 1797 Napoleon's troops were chasing the Austrians up the Brenner Pass.

Napoleon had dropped the 'u' from his surname in order to indicate that he was a Frenchman, but he showed sympathy with the Italians that he was to show to no other people, except spasmodically the Poles. He made a special point of favouring Italian scientists, as when he had the house of Volta spared during the sack of Pavia, men of letters, like those to whom he offered safe conduct out of Mantua, and painters, like Andrea Appiani (1754–1817), who became one of his favourite portraitists. Many Frenchmen who followed him, like Lucien Beyle and his brother Henri, who would later find fame as the novelist Stendhal (1783–1842), felt at ease in Italy; and Napoleon genuinely appreciated the Italian cultural achievements represented by the works of art or valuable scientific manuscripts by Leonardo da Vinci and Galileo that he grabbed. He also proved a liberal overlord of the towns he had conquered in Liguria, Lombardy and the Veneto. He objected to civil discrimination against any defined groups, as for example when he found that in the papal city of Ancona Jews had to wear the Star of David and were locked into their ghetto at night or that Muslim Greeks and Albanians were treated as second-class citizens.

His goal remained above all military and it seemed that he had gained his point when he drove the final Austrian forces back over the Dolomites. To make sure that the treaty stuck, he had ventured into the Tyrol as far as Leoben, just 80 miles from Vienna, where he concluded a truce. There he proposed a secret clause: Austria could be given Venice.

No action in the first Italian campaign was as ruthless as his treatment of the Venetian Republic, which had been careful to stay neutral until he had disappeared over the mountain passes into Austria and the Venetians, thinking he had been defeated, encouraged an uprising by the people of Verona. Napoleon hurried south and, ignoring desperate Venetian attempts at appeasement, took the city, snatched away the four horses of San Marco, the lion of St Mark and many of the most famous paintings in the world and shattered into tiny fragments the famous barge of the Doge, the *Bucentaur*, on which for centuries the head of state had been symbolically married to the sea. Napoleon was also able to claim for France the Ionian islands, including Corfu, which had been Venetian territory. Their surrender marked the end of Venice's independent existence as an imperial power.

In October 1797 the Treaty of Campo Formio followed the lines of his settlement. The Austrians recognised two new republics that he had formed, the Ligurian Republic based on Genoa and the Cisalpine Republic based on Milan. When this treaty was formalised at Rastadt, it was almost more Napoleon's triumph than France's, for north of the Alps the French under Jean Moreau (1763–1813) had done less well, until at last, just as Napoleon was concluding the truce of Leoben, Moreau crossed the Rhine and so convinced the Austrians that they must make peace. At the end Moreau's actions had helped Napoleon, but rightly Napoleon took all the glory.

He had exploited his advantages with great ability. Thanks to Gribeauval's reforms in the 1770s and 1780s, French field guns had been standardised into three main calibres, 12-, 8- and 4-pounders. They were lighter because barrels had been shortened, their wheels were larger and the guns more securely attached to their carriages, making French artillery more reliable, more powerful and more mobile than that of any other power. Napoleon had another advantage. He led a nationally cohesive army against the diverse ranks of the Austrian army. It was however his tactics that proved decisive. What mattered most was not that he made mistakes, which he did, but that he could recover from them. It was disconcerting for opposing generals to find that they could not tell when the next French division would arrive on the battlefield, from which pass or across which ford or bridge they would be attacked. The new man was too fast and too unpredictable.

With each success Napoleon and his men became more adventurous. He had first noticed the future marshal, Jean Lannes (1769–1809), leading grenadiers in a ferocious charge at Lodi. A few months later with only a few staff officers Lannes galloped up to a force of papal cavalry numbering several hundreds. 'Surrender!' he cried out; and to his amazement they did.

Napoleon had also been lucky. The only major army he had faced had been Austrian and for a long time the Austrians had concentrated on the war in the Rhineland. Since 1795 two more formidable military powers, Prussia and Russia, had been preoccupied with devouring between them the last remaining portions of the once huge kingdom of Poland. In 1796–7 they were still suffering from problems of digestion. Besides, Prussia was no longer ruled by its general-king Frederick the Great (1712–86) and in Russia the Tsarina Catherine the Great had been succeeded by her erratic son Paul (1754–1801). The only other power that counted was Britain, which could mount the occasional amphibious raid in the Netherlands or Italy or a remote part of France, but could not yet challenge a well-led French army on land.

It is possible to explain Napoleon's early successes in terms of a Napoleonic system of war. Napoleon was not an original military thinker but he was remarkably adept at seeing how what he had learned in theory could be carried out in practice. On strategy he followed first principles: to follow one objective; to make that objective the destruction of the enemy army; to place his army on the enemy's flank and rear; to turn the enemy's most exposed flank; and to keep his own lines of communication open and safe. Napoleon had three chief ways of preparing for a battle. First, no less than 30 times between 1796 and 1815 he executed the *manoeuvre sur les derrières*, a method of enveloping the enemy, so that the enemy felt trapped and was forced to fight his way out of the trap – or to surrender. Secondly, Napoleon would seek a central position from which he could attack whichever section of the enemy's army seemed the weakest. Thirdly, he might make a dash for some strategic objective to put the enemy off balance. His overall aim was always to win battles and campaigns as quickly as possible.

The French army, so ill disciplined and enthusiastic in the early years of the Revolutionary wars, was made by Napoleon into a formidable fighting machine, in which enthusiasm was always directed into winning ways. By using the system of corps, Napoleon created a whole series of mini-armies, each one of which had its artillery, infantry and cavalry component. Such units could often hold off much larger, more specialised, enemy units. But none of this would work without the overseeing eye of Napoleon, who would judge at what moment which unit should attack, where it should attack, how various attacks would be co-ordinated. After the campaigns of 1796–7 Napoleon had a psychological advantage over his enemies that he kept until 1812 or even 1813: they expected to lose and he expected to win.

When Napoleon arrived back in Paris, he was a national hero. He was already beginning to be obsessed by Britain. Early in 1798 he was given the post of commander of the Army against England. Britain was the country that in 1793 had constructed a coalition against France and its revolution by allying with Russia, Sardinia, Spain, Naples, Prussia, Austria, Portugal and, after the Holy Roman Empire had declared war, small German states such as Baden and Hesse. Five years later, the coalition, which relied on English money for its continuance, had disintegrated because of French victories or the desire to concentrate on matters other than the iniquities of a country that had vowed to export revolution. England was the only country still at war with France, but England remained untouched.

A tour of the northern French coastline convinced Napoleon that a direct invasion would be too dangerous. The previous year the English navy had routed Spanish and Dutch fleets, by then allied to France, and Lazare Hoche's attempt to land in Ireland in 1796–7 had ended in failure. A bolder scheme was necessary. In Italy Napoleon had already talked about another idea to Talleyrand, the ex-aristocrat, ex-bishop who was now Foreign Minister. Why not attack Egypt, they wondered? Egypt controlled access to India, where both France and England had had commercial interests since the 17th century but where England was now the dominant European trader. India was becoming Britain's most valuable colony. Besides, the French had a potential ally in the south of the subcontinent, the Sultan of Mysore, Tipu Sahib (1749–99), who was determined to drive out the British based in Madras.

In the minds of people in Paris Napoleon could do what he liked, but he had to be cautious. Because the government was short of cash, he demanded only a modest number of men, 25,000 (eventually he got 38,000), and he planned to be economical in his use of guns and ammunition. He chose his fellow generals carefully. One appointment, that of Louis Charles Desaix (1768–1800), turned out to be particularly fortunate, as Desaix was both inventive and loyal. The Directory granted Napoleon the services of the Mediterranean fleet from Toulon to transport the expeditionary force and to protect its lines of communication, but popular sentiment was not concerned with practicalities. What captured people's imagination was his request to be accompanied by mathematicians, physicists, biologists, botanists, linguists (above all Arabists), printers, musicians and artists.

Alexander the Great, who had been educated by Aristotle, inspired by Homer and accompanied by learned men, had once conquered Egypt. Napoleon had a similar combination of realistic and visionary qualities to that which had made Alexander an envoy of Hellenic values as well as a terrifying enemy. Napoleon had no doubt that he was going to Egypt as an envoy of civilization (a new French word for a new French concept), but he was also willing to learn. On his way out to Egypt he read a translation of the Koran and pronounced himself impressed.

True conquests, **Napoleon** said, *are those achieved over ignorance.*[15] To lead the experts in Egypt he chose Gaspard Monge (1746–1818), inventor of descriptive geometry, and Claude Louis Berthollet (1748–1822), a chemist. He later made Monge a senator and Count of Pelusium (after the Egyptian border town) and Berthollet vice-president of the Senate.

Napoleon was fortunate that he was at first able to keep his purposes secret from the English, who had temporarily abandoned the Mediterranean and, when they returned there, stopped short at Gibraltar, from where at first they aimed merely to blockade the straits and prevent the Toulon fleet from sailing into the Atlantic. But English intelligence soon revealed what was happening, and Nelson was sent to watch Toulon. It was therefore largely by luck that the French got away and linked up with other ships based at Genoa and Civitavecchia in the Papal states.

The one circumstance that caused Napoleon regret was Joséphine's failure to accompany him. Whatever the reason she had gone north to Lorraine to take the waters instead of turning south for Naples, once in Lorraine a balcony collapsed under her, injuring her so that she was in no state to join him. By then Napoleon had captured Malta (for a time) and was making the last leg of his sea journey, crossing to Alexandria, under threat from the English fleet. On 1 July he was anchored off the former capital, built by the Macedonian Ptolemies who succeeded Alexander.

By 1798 Alexandria had decayed to a dirty, depressed port, which Napoleon quickly captured and did not allow his men to sack. Curiously Napoleon made one obvious error that he would repeat in Russia in 1812 – he had not thought about the weather. The troops who had found the Lombard plain almost intolerable in summer were going to suffer much more in the Egyptian desert at the same time of year. As often he demanded near-perfect behaviour from the imperfect men who followed him; it is a sign of his remarkable hold over them that he contrived to make them do what he wanted. Desaix's troops had to march for three days through the desert to reach the Nile, while after a successful naval skirmish in the Nile that was decided when the French artillery blew up the Egyptian flagship, Napoleon's army had neared Cairo by 21 July. In the distance they could make out the Pyramids glimmering in the heat. Napoleon is reported to have said, *forty centuries* looked down on his men.[16]

The Egyptians in their multicoloured robes, with scimitars glinting in the sun and mounted on noble Arab horses, looked much more romantic than the French in their dusty, often ragged uniforms, but there was no real contest. Not for the first time a non-European army, however courageous, could not cope with superior European technology and discipline. The French were drawn up in squares, at which the Egyptian cavalry charged in vain. As for the Egyptian infantry, it had no experience of the

The French engage the Mamelukes at the battle of the Pyramids

overwhelming firepower provided by the French heavy guns. Many were killed trying to escape by swimming across the Nile, which ran red with their blood. The battle was over within two hours.

The route was open to Cairo, the Memphis of the Pharaohs, the capital of lower Egypt, the city that under the Arabs had replaced Alexandria as capital and cultural centre of the whole country. The city's glorious medieval days were past. Since the Turks had conquered Egypt the practical government of the country was left in the hands of Mamelukes, professional soldiers from the Muslim regions of either Albania or Circassia, the land between the Crimea and the Caucasus mountains. The only fine buildings left in Cairo were a few mosques and palaces and much of the city was squalid, but it was from here that Napoleon would govern and spread civilisation to the whole country. He gave power to an Egyptian divan of nine elders to be advised by a French commissioner and then set off to maul Mamelukes who had fled into the Sinai desert.

The solitary Napoleon considers the Sphinx. An engraving from a painting by J L Gerome

On his return he received bad news. Nelson had caught up with the French fleet off Aboukir and, after placing some of his ships between the French ships and the shore, had attacked them from both sides and annihilated them. The French, now without a fleet, were cut off from France.

Napoleon did not despair. He set up a postal service and a mint to change Egyptian into French currency; he had watermills and windmills built; he established a hospital for the poor; he set about mapping lower Egypt; he put lights in the main streets; and he funded the country's first printing press using Arabic type. He discussed religion with the muftis and declared that at heart he and his soldiers were Muslims too. The muftis saw problems: were his men circumcised and would they abstain from wine? Napoleon paused. The muftis, however, were prepared to declare that Napoleon was a friend of the Prophet and Napoleon celebrated Mohammed's birthday with parades, fireworks and salutes. He got his learned men to investigate the chemistry of the salty lakes of Libya, to measure the proportions of the sphinx, to find out the causes of ophthalmia, an inflammation of the eye common in the country, and to watch crocodiles, ibises and a primitive genus of snake-like fish, named *polypterus* by one of Napoleon's zoologists. When he dispatched Desaix to chase the Mamelukes who were withdrawing into upper Egypt, he sent the artist Vivant Denon (1747–1825) to sketch the ancient buildings; and so Denon witnessed the moment when the soldiers caught sight of the huge temples of Karnak near Thebes, the ancient capital of upper Egypt, and burst out cheering.

In the winter of 1798–9, Napoleon's love life was again giving him cause for concern. He had been deprived of the company of women and when he heard through Junot, who had been a witness of their affair in the carriage on the way to Italy, that Joséphine was still being unfaithful with Hippolyte Charles, Napoleon was initially distraught. Then he decided to pay her back. He wanted to make sure that his adultery would be talked about. After looking around for a good-looking lover his eye lighted on Pauline Fourès, 20-year-old wife of a young lieutenant. He spilt coffee over her at a dinner party and suggested she should retire to a private room to clean up. He followed her there and they did not emerge for two hours. This affair lasted several months, but poor Pauline was only a weapon in a private war.

Public warfare was a more pressing concern. Knowing that, as the Turks had declared war, they were going to attack him in Egypt, he determined to strike first. A naval force would take some time to arrive, but the military force that the Turks had assembled in Syria could arrive quickly. Napoleon marched his army out from Cairo. On 25 February he took Gaza and 2,000 prisoners, on 7 May Jaffa and 4,000 prisoners. As many of the second lot of men had been freed at Gaza on the assurance that they would not fight against the French again, he decided they could not be trusted and on 10 May had them shot. He was becoming as brutal as a Turk.

In the end it was formidable Crusader fortifications that stopped him. At the Syrian fortified port of Acre he confronted British sailors under Commodore Sir William Sidney Smith (1764–1840), the royalist Phélipeaux, whom he had hated at the Ecole Militaire and who now prepared the defences as a British officer, and a tough old Bosnian, Ahmed Djezzar, from the Turkish dominion in the Balkans, who promised he would take no prisoners. Though Napoleon won another victory in fields beneath Mount Tabor, the site where traditionally Christ had been transfigured before his disciples, and though his troops were received with joy by Christian Arabs in Nazareth, the village where Christ had passed his childhood, he could not penetrate the walls of Acre before a Turkish force arrived by sea to relieve the besieged city. In the last years of his life, in exile on St Helena, Napoleon would count this defeat in Syria as one of the great frustrations of his career. But for that *I would have reached Constantinople and the Indies*, he said. *I would have changed the face of the world.*[17]

Reluctantly he withdrew and, leaving many wounded behind him in Jaffa, hastened back to Egypt, in time to meet a Turkish army, which had just landed on the shore at Aboukir. Once more, however, his troops were too quick for his flamboyant enemies, thousands of whom drowned, as the French attacked them on the beach. *This battle*, he told Murat hyperbolically, *will decide the fate of the world.*[18]

What did decide the world's fate, at least for the next 15 years, was the news he got from France. France was already having to fight the Austrians and Neapolitans as well as the Turks and the British; now there was a new enemy, the Russians, who were everywhere, with armies in the Netherlands, Switzerland and Italy and with a fleet off Corfu. Talleyrand sent word that Napoleon could return if he left someone else in charge. He left that frightening responsibility to General Jean-Baptiste Kléber (1753–1800) and prepared to embark. He must have known that without a fleet to bring supplies there was no way out for the majority of Frenchmen who were left behind. In the end Kléber did not face the consequences, because he was assassinated, and it was his successor, Jacques-François Menou (1750–1810), who in 1801 surrendered to a British force. In 1811 a survivor from the land battle of Aboukir, an Albanian called Mehmet Ali, massacred the Mameluke leaders, making himself and his heirs the effective rulers of Egypt down to the time of his dissolute descendant, Farouk.

The Egyptian Institute, modelled on a similar organisation in Paris, worked hard to produce an encyclopaedic account of Egypt, its buildings, races, geography, industry and agriculture. It took until 1828 for the *Description de l'Egypte* to be published, but preliminary work was done long before Napoleon lost power and he took some sheets with him to St Helena to remind him of a glorious venture.

The French also discovered a key document of Ptolemaic Egypt, the Rosetta Stone, buried in mud in the Nile delta. The officer who retrieved it realised it was covered in three kinds of writing: Greek, priestly Egyptian, which became known as hieroglyphics, and demotic or popular Egyptian. The French commander Menou kept it under his bed. He had to give it up when he surrendered to the British, and it was placed in the British Museum. Jean-François Champollion (1790–1832), a young French archaeologist who had mastered Coptic, the language descended from Ancient Egyptian, was able, using a copy, to crack the stone's code by deciphering its hieroglyphs. Thanks to him the chance discovery of a damaged slab of black basalt led to the creation of Egyptology.

In one solitary frigate Napoleon and a few chosen companions made the difficult journey to France, dodging the British till they docked at Fréjus. From there he hastened back to Paris. He was going to make Joséphine pay for her infidelity. She, frightened of the results of her own folly, set out to meet him but missed him. He arrived at their home in the rue Chatereine and locked himself in their bedroom. She needed the supportive tears of her children before he would unlock the door to let her in. Eventually he gave way, but their relationship had changed for good. He was now the undisputed master and she never dared to contradict him again. As for Hippolyte Charles, he had to go; and he kept silent until his death.

France's problems were less easy to solve. It was obvious to some reformers that the Directorate, with all its inbuilt indecisiveness, was inadequate for the crises international warfare involved. Napoleon was the one man who could act as a saviour, but in spite of his experiences in Italy and in Egypt he was not a trained administrator. Barras, Napoleon's former protector, wanted his protégé out of the way and recommended that he resume control of the Army of Italy, but Napoleon replied that he must stay in Paris for the good of his health.

Emmanuel-Joseph Sieyès (1748–1836), a former priest, political theorist and now a Director, had ideas about how France should be run in a way that was more workable than the 1795 constitution that set up the Directory. Looking around for allies to help him destroy the system, he approached Napoleon. Sieyès assumed that Napoleon would carry out the *coup d'état*, from which Sieyès would benefit – but the issue was left unclear.

On the morning of 17 November (18 Brumaire, the foggy month), Sieyès persuaded the senior chamber, the Ancients, that there was so much danger of a Jacobin plot that they should leave the Tuileries palace for the palace of Saint-Cloud outside Paris. After that it was comparatively easy to persuade the junior chamber, the Five Hundred, that they should do likewise. Away from the crowds of the capital they were vulnerable to the military powers of persuasion or so it must have seemed to Napoleon when, having adroitly tricked most of the Directors into resigning, in one case by lying that Barras had resigned, and, having had the two who refused to resign arrested, he tried to force the chambers to give up the following day. He surrounded the palace of Saint-

Cloud with 6,000 soldiers, and, growing nervous and impatient, burst in on the Ancients' deliberations to announce that conspirators were plotting against them. Challenged, he could not name anyone, blustered and was advised to withdraw. Would the troops be loyal to him or to the Republic as it was? In the end it was the tongue of his brother Lucien, President of the Five Hundred, that saved the day. He painted a lurid picture of assassins in the pay of England waiting to kill his brother. The guards advanced into the palace, most of those belonging to either chamber fled and a rump voted for a new order that would be headed by Napoleon, Sieyès and an ally and friend of Napoleon's called Ducos. By the end of the day it was obvious that France would have its new constitution and that one of the key figures in the new France would be Napoleon.

On the day of the crisis Napoleon had almost failed, but in subsequent days he showed more characteristic political skill. Within a few days he had made himself the leading political figure in France. His reign had begun.

The First Consul 1799–1804

Even though Napoleon was involved, it took a few weeks to work out the details of a new constitution. Sieyès believed in government by assemblies, Napoleon in government by Napoleon. Sieyès resigned his post as provisional 'consul', a title he had taken from the ancient Romans, and suggested that Napoleon should call himself Grand Elector, a title Napoleon declined. Instead he kept on calling long meetings at night to resolve the problems, until his critics were so exhausted that they agreed that there should be three consuls, of whom the first would have executive powers and two others would be advisers. Napoleon then asked Sieyès to nominate the three consuls and Sieyès chose Napoleon, Jean-Jacques Régis Cambacérès (1753–1824), a former Jacobin, and Charles-François Lebrun (1739–1824), a former royalist. These proposals were then submitted to a referendum. Of an electorate of more than 9,000,000 (every adult male) over 3,000,000 voted in favour and just over 1,500 against (in Paris only 10 against). Napoleon's careful nurturing of his public image – the bulletins that he sent home from his campaigns in Italy and Egypt, the victory parades – had paid off. Lucien, now Minister of the Interior, rounded up votes from the departments and added half a million for the Army on the grounds that it must favour Napoleon. For the first time since 1789 France had a leader who had the power to be strong.

Napoleon had come to power because he seemed to be a general

Napoleon as First Consul in a portrait by Philips

of unequalled gifts, the only man always capable of saving France from her enemies. When he left Egypt, those enemies had threatened to take away all the lands that France had gained since 1792. By the end of 1798, however, the situation was a little less grave. The indispensable Massena, already a seasoned general before he served under Napoleon in Italy, had defeated a Russian army at the battle of Zürich in September 1798 and thus secured the Swiss or Helvetic Republic as a puppet state that helpfully separated the Austrian territories in Germany from the territories they had regained in Italy. Meanwhile the new Tsar had left the coalition against France. Tsar Paul I, an emotional ruler prone to self-doubt, trusted in Napoleon to give him confidence. The Russian ruler organised a Baltic alliance against the English, whose habit of stopping and searching neutral shipping made them hated by other seafaring powers. But all the alliance achieved was to provoke Nelson into destroying the Danish navy at anchor in Copenhagen, leaving the Tsar's Baltic allies still more at the mercy of the British.

Russia's withdrawal left Napoleon with just one important enemy on land, the inevitable Austrians. His first idea was a bold thrust across the Rhine as a first step *en route* to Vienna via southern Germany, but the well-established General Moreau persuaded him to proceed more cautiously. While Moreau advanced slowly into Germany on a broad front, Napoleon switched his main attack to Italy, where the French had lost all their conquests, except for the Ligurian coastline around Genoa, during his time in Egypt. The Austrians decided to launch their own onslaught there. Soon Massena was pent up in Genoa, where he had to face the Austrians on land and the British at sea. He could not hold out beyond the beginning of June, so Napoleon had to be quick. He was expected to edge his way along the coast road, but chose instead to take the shorter, much more perilous route over the St Bernard Pass. To bypass one Austrian post, he dragged cannon across straw and dung at night, but there were more mishaps than he admitted. Too many guns, men and horses went over too many precipices and, when he reached the lower reaches, he was ill-equipped to fight a prolonged campaign.

Napoleon, who was obsessed with luck, would prove to be very lucky now. By deciding not to march on Genoa immediately and leaving Massena to his fate, he gave himself a chance to carry out one of his favourite manoeuvres: putting his own forces between his enemy's army and its base. He reached Milan and then waited for his elderly Austrian opponent to panic. Michael Melas (1729–1806), who was besieging Massena in Genoa, may have been yet another old Austrian general but he was not stupid. For the moment he did nothing. He had been expecting a battle, which was likely to occur on one or other side of the Po. Napoleon detached Desaix, his Egyptian comrade, with two divisions, to block Melas's route south and prevent him from getting to the Po and so the Lombard plain. He was sure that Melas would not cross the Bormida, a tiny river that meandered between his own and the Austrian's forces, but Melas had by now gone on the offensive, fearing that Napoleon would soon join up with another French army under Massena and Suchet. Napoleon was taken aback when his 22,000 men and their 14 guns suddenly found themselves faced with an Austrian army of 30,000 men with 100 guns that had crossed the Bormida at dawn. Napoleon had to fight, as he had intended, but at a disadvantage, which he had not planned.

According to the official accounts of the battle, the Austrians advanced four times and were thrown back four times before they eventually forced the French right to retreat. It looked as if the rest would be overwhelmed, until Melas at last showed his age. Slightly wounded, he retired for a catnap. At this stage, according to the official version, 'the presence of the First Consul revived the morale of the troops'. What had really revived morale was the sudden and unexpected return of Desaix from the south. Desaix at once counter-attacked, threw the Austrians into disarray and made them vulnerable to a decisive French cavalry charge. As Desaix was killed at this moment of triumph, Napoleon was not obliged to share his good fortune with anyone. Though he always maintained that the battle of Marengo was one of the closest he ever fought, that did not prevent him from steadily making his own part in it more and more masterly. The forced retreats became cunning

A triumphant Napoleon presents the Sword of Honour to his Grenadiers after the battle of Marengo

ploys to draw the enemy into a trap and the fortuitous appearance of Desaix a sign of Napoleon's great timing. Whereas at the time Desaix seems to have said, 'we have lost one battle; let us win another,'[19] when Napoleon was dictating his memoirs on St Helena Desaix was made to say, 'our affairs are going badly, the battle is lost, I can guarantee only the retreat, can't I?' to which

Napoleon is supposed to have replied, *On the contrary, as far as I am concerned, the battle has never been in doubt ... Push your column forwards, you have only to pluck the fruits of your victory.*[20]

Melas was too disheartened to carry on with the struggle and quickly asked for and was granted an armistice. In Milan Napoleon acquired a new mistress, a soprano named Giuseppina Grassini, before hurrying back to Paris to explain how he had won back northern Italy. The defeat of Austria was certain only when Moreau had conquered at Hohenlinden in 1801 and moved close to Vienna. The Austrians could not continue. In the treaty of Lunéville, signed on 8 February 1801, Austria was left with Venice. The duchy of Parma, which the French had strategic interest in, was absorbed into their puppet Cisalpine republic, in return for which the duke of Parma acquired Tuscany, and the Duke of Tuscany was awarded Salzburg and Bechtoldsgaden.

Such shuffling of land was a normal feature of European diplomacy: what was a Napoleonic feature were the massive French gains. Napoleon was both a tough negotiator and an intimidating opponent. The Rhine became the eastern border of France and the Dutch, Swiss, Ligurian and Cisalpine republics, all French creations and puppets, were recognised, so that France replaced Austria in northern Italy and encroached on Austria's area of influence in Germany. In southern Italy, however, France was less rigorously anti-monarchical, allowing the King of Naples back. The public face of France was republican, the private reality imperial.

There remained one enemy undefeated, now as ready for peace as France. In 1801 the belligerent Prime Minister Pitt had resigned, to be replaced by the more amenable Henry Addington (1757–

Giuseppina Grassini (1773–1850) was just one among the actresses and singers who came to Napoleon's bed. She was noticed in Milan, then installed in a house in Paris, but sent back after being found with a violinist. Napoleon, she said, was her lover too late. Earlier, her charms had been irresistible.

1844). If France would leave Naples, then the British would leave Malta, which they had taken when Napoleon left the island for Egypt. Egypt would go back to France. The English had in fact at the time of their negotiations just defeated the French there but, while Napoleon, thanks to better intelligence, knew it, the English did not. Peace was signed in October 1801 and March 1802 at Amiens, but both sides must have known that what they had settled for was merely a truce.

Napoleon used the peace to send General Leclerc (1772–1802), the first husband of his sister Pauline, to subdue Saint-Domingue, one-third of the Caribbean island of Hispaniola, where the blacks had achieved a perturbing degree of self-rule. Between 1801 and 1803 all but 12 per cent of the French troops sent to take this freedom away died of yellow fever, Leclerc among them; and the remnant surrendered to the British. Napoleon's men had tried to put down the revolt with great brutality and the slaves' leader, Toussaint L'Ouverture (c1743–1803), was seized and brought to France to die in a French prison, But in November and December 1803, the French troops were decisively defeated, paving the way for **Napoleon came to think** his Saint-Domingue policy foolish. *I should have treated with the black chiefs like the authorities in a province, named black officers in their race's regiments, left Toussaint Louverture as viceroy, sent no troops.* [21]

Saint-Domingue's declaration of independence on 1 January 1804, under the new name of Haiti. Napoleon decided to abandon his plans for the New World. In 1803 he sold France's claims to the vast swathe of territory known as Louisiana, which covered the whole area of the Mississippi basin, to the American president, Thomas Jefferson (1743–1826). The sale tacitly acknowledged that in the race to be the dominant global power France had already lost out to Britain. From then on Napoleon would concentrate on France's ambitions to be the dominant European power on the continent.

If France was to play that role then it must become a better organised country. The Consulate was marked by a determined effort to adapt France to its new circumstances. The Revolution, as Napoleon liked to say, was over. What he saw must follow was the construction of a post-revolutionary society. Once his own role as First Consul had been defined, as vaguely as possible, he set about extending his powers over France. By the law of 28 Pluviôse of Year VIII (17 February 1800) he acquired the power to appoint the leading officials in each department: the prefect, the general council that dealt with the budget, the prefecture council that ruled in administrative disputes, and the subprefects who managed the sub-divisions of the department, known as districts or *arrondissements*. In this way he established the bureaucracy that has kept France in order up to the present day. He left much of the business of choosing suitable prefects to the Second and Third Consuls. Cambacérès, the ex-Convention politician from the south, nominated eight prefects in the south. Lebrun, the ex-royalist from Normandy, nominated ten prefects in the east, around Paris and in the conservative west.

In his search for bureaucrats Napoleon was willing to employ anyone who was competent, whether they had been faithful to Louis XVI or had voted for his death. The same pragmatic princi-ples inspired his project to codify the law. This was a task that had been adumbrated during the revolutionary decade of 1789–99, as it became obvious that many of the changes that had given France a new uniformity of structure implied a new legal uniformity. In the north property rights were determined by Teutonic custom, in the south by Roman principles according to the 6th-century code of the Greek Emperor Justinian. The abolition of feudal rights, renounced in August 1789, and the nationalisation of Church property, voted in November 1789, meant that all over France titles to property had to be redefined. Similarly, as Church law no longer laid down the norms for the regulation of marriage, it was necessary to draw out the implications of the new system of civil marriage.

Napoleon liked to think of himself as the driving force behind the drafting of the new Civil Code and he did show his mastery in leading the experts to quick decisions, but much of the work required a technical expertise that he lacked. Occasionally his Corsican attitudes to the family and to women determined the result of the discussions. He had no doubt that a man was the natural head of the family, who could tell his wife what to do, but, if divorce became necessary for the good of the family, he preferred that it should occur by mutual consent. Needless to say, it did not occur to him that one day he might be glad to have the right to divorce.

The Civil Code was but the first of a series of new codes that covered the main categories of law. Though Napoleon sponsored the creation of these laws, he had neither the time nor the expertise to be directly involved in their construction.

In one area of French life the quest for uniformity had been disastrous. In 1790 the deputies of the National Assembly had decided that 'the people' should take over the Church itself, so that the Church would be coterminous with the nation. There would be one bishop for every department; and, like the men who ran the secular business of the departments, those responsible for the clerical business should be elected too. As members of the intelligentsia of the age, the Assembly members presumed that no thoughtful person was likely to dissent from the concept of one civic religion; and many representatives of the lower clergy had been enthusiastic supporters of the idea of a National Assembly and made no objections as the privileges of the upper clergy were abolished. But, though there was a long tradition of independence in the French church, it remained fundamentally Catholic and so in communion with the Pope. Pius VI (1717–99) had tried to avoid falling out with the new regime in France but the Assembly made no effort to accommodate his scruples. Eventually in April 1791 Pius VI condemned the so-called Civil Constitution and suspended clergy who had taken an oath of loyalty to it. Many priests refused to take the oath and the hesitant Louis XVI finally made up his mind and refused to condemn them. By the end of 1791 France had two parallel churches: a constitutional one, approved by the State, and a 'refractory' one, faithful to the Pope.

As the revolution grew more radical, religion became even more divisive. Though the people of the Vendée region had objected originally to conscription, they soon showed that they hated the regime that wanted to make them fight above all because it was anti-Catholic and anti-royalist. Only a bloody campaign subdued them.

Nearly ten years later, the religious situation in France had become the reverse of the revolutionary ideal of civic unity. Protestants and Jews found themselves better treated while Catholics, the majority of French Christians, were made to suffer. If the government regarded the Catholic Church as inevitably counter-revolutionary, then there was a link between loyalty to the Crown and loyalty to the Pope.

Napoleon wanted to separate France from its kings. When the Comte de Lille (1755–1824), elder surviving brother of Louis XVI and the future Louis XVIII, wrote to congratulate him on his new title, Napoleon's reply was sharp. *I thank you for your kind remarks about myself. You must give up any hope of returning to France: you would have to pass over a hundred thousand dead bodies.*[22] If he could make peace between the nation and the Church in Rome, he might detach devout Catholics from loyalty to the Bourbons.

Napoleon had prepared for this policy with his careful treatment of the Pope during the Italian campaigns, but it carried a risk of alienating the sceptical republicans, among whose ranks were numbered many of his soldiers. While Napoleon had been in Egypt, Pius VI had been brought to France, and died there. To reconcile country with Church, Napoleon would have to treat with Pius VII (1742–1823).

In the context of the time Napoleon's reconciliation with the Church was one of his most remarkable achievements. After Easter 1801 the new Pope, who had in his time seen liberty, equality and fraternity as Christian values, sent his Secretary of State, Cardinal Ercole Consalvi (1757–1824), to negotiate with the First Consul. When Consalvi wondered if he could extract more favourable terms than those he was offered, he was advised, not without reason, that in Paris the First Consul was his only ally. Napoleon did not offer much. He would not concede that the Catholic faith was the religion of France – it was the religion only of the majority of Frenchmen – nor restore the property of the Church that had been confiscated in the 1790s, nor finance seminaries to educate future clergy or any religious congregations. The future French Catholic Church would be poor. When, in April 1802, without discussing the matter with Rome, Napoleon published the so-called Organic Articles, he made it clear that in some matters, like communication with the Pope, the Church must obey the State.

As the Pope had also already conceded that the First Consul, or rather, in practice, his Minister of the Interior, would nominate bishops before the Pope appointed them, Napoleon's concordat with the Pope (signed on 15 July 1801) placed little restraint on his own authority. A combination of Napoleon's bullying and the papacy's weakness and pragmatism gave the first Consul a remarkable and eirenic victory. Many more Catholics could now accept him as leader and many émigrés returned to France. Napoleon had found it difficult at first to secure backing in Paris for his approaches to the Pope and he continued to be unsure of his position. But his victory at Marengo and his peace with Austria and Britain had gradually strengthened him sufficiently that by 1801 he was able to insist that the Legislature make the Concordat French law.

By temperament Napoleon did not like assemblies of any kind. The 1799 Constitution had established a Senate, 31 of whose

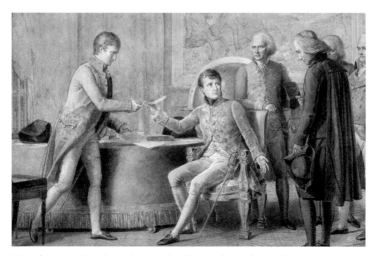

Napoleon as First Consul signs the Concordat with the Pope

members were chosen by the First Consul and 29 co-opted by the 31. This Senate chose the members of the Tribunate, which could discuss but not vote on laws, and the Legislature, which could vote on laws but not discuss them. Even so the Tribunate had turned out to be argumentative and he had found it hard to get his concordat through. This was not their function as Napoleon had conceived it.

Following an assassination attempt at the end of 1800, he had ordered the exile of a number of prominent Jacobins, even though the evidence of his own police was that the plot was fashioned by royalists, but he did not seek to eliminate all opposition to his rule until 1802. When the Senate suggested his term should be limited to ten years, he indicated that a different question should be put to the electorate: whether he, Napoleon Bonaparte, should be Consul for life. The ten-year option was ignored; and it was the first time his christian name was used as well as his surname, the first stage in the process whereby 'Napoleon' ousted 'Bonaparte'. As required, the French people gave him their usual overwhelming support. He had made peace, stabilised the economy, reached a religious agreement with the Pope and urged royalist émigrés to come back to France. The scale of his victory – 3,600,000 votes to less than 9,000 – may have been inaccurately recorded but there seems little reason to doubt that he was overwhelmingly popular. That he had been able to become a dictator seemed to worry nobody. He was the person the French wanted as their ruler and they were prepared to accept him on his own terms.

He then used his near-dictatorial status to put the politicians in their place. He divided the Tribunate into three sections, removed those tribunes he did not like and was delighted that people lost interest in tribunal debates. Meanwhile he laid down that he could give national estates (lands left over from the confiscation of Church property during the revolution) to one third of the Senators, who in this way became his most docile supporters.

Napoleon's vision of France was of a country that obeyed his every whim. In 1802 he instituted a new method of rewarding those who served him well: the Legion of Honour. For most of his rule, whether as First Consul or Emperor, most recipients of this sign of official approval were soldiers. Though Napoleon's consular reforms meant that France was well run in peacetime, the foundation of his regime remained success in war.

The most intractable issue that demanded the attention of the First Consul was finance. Before 1789 France's economic problems had been bound up with its inadequate financial arrangements. After helping the American rebels win independence from Britain, the French government had had to repay huge debts, but the existing tax system could not yield the necessary funds and France had no means of managing national debt. In 1789 the National Assembly approved a measure that gave short-term relief. Church lands were confiscated and turned into 'national goods'; and a paper currency, the so-called *assignats*, was issued against this property. The property-selling boom that followed led to a fall in the value of land and therefore of the *assignats*. France developed a dangerous case of inflation that was forgotten only because by late 1792 the new French republic was struggling for survival against the old monarchies of the continent, especially Austria and Prussia, which were backed up spasmodically by the richest country in Europe, the mercantile regime of Britain.

The Directorate, being dominated by men of business, had tried to carry out some financial reforms, but it was involved in war for all but a year and a half of its four-year existence. The regime also had a well-earned reputation for corruption, as during the Directory army contractors had done much better for themselves than for France. Napoleon quickly associated his regime with improved financial institutions. Within days of coming to power he announced the creation of a sinking fund that would control debt; and in January 1800 he established the Bank of France. The Bank did not have the far-ranging remit of a modern central bank to control the economy, but it proved to be an adequate instrument for raising money to fund government expenditure. When Napoleon needed funds after the coup of Brumaire, private bankers could produce no more than a quarter of the money they were asked for. Napoleon therefore forced Gabriel Ouvrard (1770–1846), the richest of the contractors, to surrender some of his profits and it was with this money that Napoleon set up his Bank.

In 1795 the Directorate had reintroduced a unit of currency, the franc, that had not been known since the Middle Ages, as a replacement for the traditional *livre tournois* (the Tours pound) as well as the despised *assignat*. This unit was divisible into *decimes* and *centimes*, tenths and hundredths, bringing the franc into line with the metric system, which had been first adopted in 1791. The new currency was to be metallic, an admirable aim, but one that France seemed in no condition to enforce, as the country was short of silver and gold. For a time Napoleon had been able to raid the coffers of the Netherlands – in the 18th century Amsterdam was the financial capital of Europe – but, when in 1803 Spain had to pay France 6 million francs a month for the privilege of being neutral in the forthcoming war between Britain and France, Ouvrard offered to bring piastres to France from Spain's colonies, Mexico and Cuba. When he could not fulfil his promises, he precipitated a crisis of confidence, so reinforcing Napoleon's conviction that the Bank must be tightly controlled. Military victories in 1805 and 1806 eased the financial shortfalls and France was soon able to replenish its stock of precious metals from Prussia.

As the Consulate gave France the longest period of peace between 1792 and 1815, normal commercial activity revived and it became easier to raise taxes. Napoleon chose an able former Treasury official of the pre-revolutionary government to be his Minister of Finance. Martin-Michel-Charles Gaudin (1756–1841) recorded his impression of Napoleon on their first meeting: 'He was fairly short, dressed in a grey overcoat, very thin, with a yellowish skin, the eye of an eagle and a man whose gestures were lively and animated.' Gaudin demanded that collectors of taxes should make an advance deposit of the yield they expected to collect and by the end of 1800 tax returns were up to date. Gaudin would remain Finance Minister for as long as Napoleon stayed in power and his effectiveness contributed to one of the key characteristics of Napoleon's rule. Napoleonic France never had the financial flexibility or high-risk economic dynamism that the younger William Pitt achieved in England, which made it much easier for the British government to raise loans and to lend, but Napoleon's reputation for fiscal prudence soothed the worries of French propertied and commercial interests.

Everything ultimately turned on two prerequisites: either France must avoid wars or it must win wars. Until 1812 Napoleon offered one of these two conditions of continuing prosperity. Until 1812 his rule guaranteed stability, and stability mattered more than freedom.

Emperor of the French, master of Europe
1804–7

In 1804 Napoleon indicated that being First Consul for life was not sufficiently exalted for him. He wanted to be grander than the King of Great Britain and Ireland; he wanted to be on the same level as the Holy Roman Emperor and the Tsar of all the Russias; he wanted to be the Emperor of the French.

The understanding between Britain and France had broken down by the summer of 1803. The British had hoped to revive free trade along the lines of a commercial treaty that Pitt's government had made long ago with France in 1786. Napoleon knew that that treaty had devastated France's textile industry; so he would not revive it. Napoleon's diplomatic manoeuvres increased British mistrust. Though he withdrew troops from Naples and the Papal States, he was slow to leave the Netherlands, annexed Piedmont and the isle of Elba, and occupied Parma. He imposed a federal structure on Switzerland, now the Helvetic Republic, and renamed the Cisalpine Republic as the Italian Republic and made himself its President. When Lord Whitworth (1752–1825), Britain's ambassador, was sent to Paris in November 1802, he was told not to mention the disputed island of Malta, which Britain showed no sign of relinquishing. The French official newspaper, *Le Moniteur*, discussed how many troops might be needed to reconquer Egypt, so that the gullible Whitworth sent reports home that the French were thinking of returning to the East.

The British Foreign Secretary approached the Russians to ask if they would help resist French aggression. Russia had had a new Tsar since 1801, when a group of nobles in English pay had murdered Paul I, who had become an ally of Napoleon. His son, Alexander I (1777–1825), who was an accessory to the murder and emotionally vulnerable through guilt, was even more anxious than his father to cut a dash on the European scene, but, since neither he nor his country was ready, he refused Britain's request.

In mid-March 1803 Napoleon turned on Whitworth in the presence of other ambassadors, but it was not until the British had rejected Napoleon's offer of a deal over Malta (he had suggested that the British occupy the island for three years before the Russians took over) that Whitworth left Paris in mid-May. Napoleon marched into Hanover, the continental kingdom of George III, and interned some young Englishmen of military age; the British seized French ships. These were but the opening salvoes. While the French thought of how to land troops on British soil, in August the British did land a small group of royalists on French soil. The plotters were arrested; one man who was actually willing to negotiate with their leader turned out to be Moreau, the victor of Hohenlinden. The royalists were condemned to death, Moreau exiled. Napoleon was sure that he should strike at the Bourbon royal family. Unreliable intelligence indicated that the young Duke of Enghien (1772–1804), heir to the Prince de Condé (1736–1818), was behind the conspiracy. Enghien was seized from his refuge in Baden, unjustly tried and unjustly executed. Napoleon's actions shocked many who had been willing to admire him, like the young aristocrat François-René de Chateaubriand (1768–1848), recently returned from exile. There could now be no peace between Bonapartes and Bourbons. In these circumstances the Senate announced that Napoleon would become hereditary Emperor.

It was not hard to arrange the necessary votes to show that the

French people rejoiced in this new prospective title – he called a plebiscite and won it by an overwhelming margin – but Napoleon's ambition was not limited to a mere name. He wanted to accede to his new honour in the presence of the Pope and so invited Pius VII come to Paris in November. Some of the cardinals advised Pius to say no, but the Pope hoped for some relaxation of the Organic Articles. He went, but found he could not speak to Napoleon on important matters of principle; and when the ceremony was acted out in Notre-Dame on 2 December 1804, his role was close to an insult.

Like a Caesar when France was Gaul, Napoleon wore laurel leaves; in portraits he holds the sceptre of an early 7th-century king of the Franks, Dagobert. The closest comparisons in the French or Frankish past were with the Pope crowning Charlemagne in 800 as the first western Emperor and with the journey of an earlier Pope in the mid-8th century across the Alps to seek the protection of Charlemagne's father. Napoleonic propaganda linked his assumption of his new role to obscure events in the remoter Middle Ages, while ignoring the fact that the French royal houses had ruled securely in an unbroken line for most of the thousand years that had supervened. It was all too clear that, compared to French kings, the new Emperor was an upstart.

The imperial coronation departed from the past in some significant ways. In the past Frankish and French kings had been anointed with oil and crowned in Reims cathedral, then taken communion. The first of these ceremonies was adapted to Napoleon's needs, so that the Pope anointed his head, arms and shoulders but then watched while Napoleon crowned himself and then Joséphine. Napoleon did not take communion. The Pope had already accepted these changes. Someone, probably Joséphine, then alerted him to the fact that the Emperor and Empress had not had a Christian marriage, so he insisted that they should have. Hurriedly and privately they made their vows before Napoleon's

A detail from Jacques-Louis David's painting of the coronation of Napoleon

uncle Cardinal Fesch, vows which, alas, had no binding force in modern, Napoleonic law.

Napoleon's *parvenu* Empire now required grandeur. While he had been in Egypt, Josephine had bought a house outside Paris at Malmaison, which a pair of architect designers, Charles Percier and Pierre-François-Léonard Fontaine had altered and decorated. When Napoleon became First Consul he took to living in the Tuileries Palace in the centre of Paris, where he instructed the same pair to provide him with a magnificent setting. Although he also had them make the neighbouring Louvre home to the Musée Napoléon, the grandest collection of art in western Europe, Napoleon's chief concern was that the Tuileries should be worthy of his regime. As most of the Tuileries palace was burnt down in 1871, we know what was achieved only from old engravings and paintings, but the elegant arch of Percier and Fontaine's Arc du Carrousel, the smart rue de Rivoli and the vista that leads the eye first towards place de la Concorde, then up the Champs Elysées to the Arc de Triomphe at Etoile conveys that sense of majesty Napoleon wished to create at the heart of his imperial capital.

Charles Percier (1764–1834) and Pierre-François-Léonard Fontaine (1762–1853) were partners and Napoleon's favourite architects and designers. But having experienced how expensive Joséphine's purchase and refurbishment of Malmaison had been, he was determined not to pay them too much. *Architects*, he said, *ruined Louis XIV because the great king could not count.*[23]

Meanwhile, the principal political task facing Napoleon was how to react to the resumption of war with Britain, where Pitt had been back in charge since 1804. The thought of invading Britain from northern France fascinated the new emperor. Julius Caesar had done it and, as he reminded the Parisians when he exhibited the Bayeux Tapestry at the Louvre, so had William the Conqueror. He dreamed of assembling two forces of landing craft at Dunkirk and Cherbourg, which would rendezvous at Boulogne; he thought about the kinds of boat needed to carry guns and horses; he maintained that the Channel was just a ditch to be leapt over; he was confident that he required only one calm night while every British ship was miles and miles away.

In spring 1804 he gave instructions to the admiral of the

Toulon fleet, Louis-René Latouche-Tréville (1745–1804) to elude Nelson's blockade of the Mediterranean, link up with the Rochefort fleet commanded by Pierre de Villeneuve (1763–1806) and join the flotilla at the narrowest part of the Channel. Sadly in August Latouche-Tréville died and the plan was shelved, only to be revived once Spain declared war on Britain in December 1804. This time Villeneuve, now switched to Toulon, was given the job of escaping into the Atlantic, heading for Martinique in the Caribbean, joining up with the Spaniards and then, on his return into European waters, linking up with the ships based at Rochefort, Brest and Ferrol. Napoleon continued to pace the Channel cliffs.

Villeneuve set sail at the end of March 1805, evaded the watching Nelson in the Mediterranean – Nelson thought the French wished to attack Sicily, Malta or Egypt – and headed for the open ocean. He got back to European waters ahead of Nelson but the Royal Navy prevented him from getting north of Corunna. Napoleon gave him instructions that, if need be, he should move south to Cadiz and there join up, not with other French ships, but with the Spanish fleet. On 24 August Napoleon gave orders that the Army of Boulogne should move away from the French coast to the Danube, effectively abandoning his invasion plans, but he did not change Villeneuve's instructions. Less than two months later, at the battle of Trafalgar, Nelson so completely crushed the combined French and Spanish fleets that no European nation was in a position to challenge British control of European waters until the end of the century.

In May 1805 in Milan Napoleon had been crowned King of all Italy. His 'Italy' may not have included Naples or even, then, the whole of the Papal States, but he had changed the Italian Republic into his personal kingdom, over which his step-son Eugène de Beauharnais ruled as Viceroy. In June 1805, he broke the Treaty of Lunéville by annexing Genoa to France. In August the Austrians retaliated by allying themselves with Britain and Russia against France, forming the Third Coalition. The British and the Russians had already signed a convention to restrict French gains since the treaty of Amiens; now Austria signed it too. Napoleon found convenient allies in three medium-sized German states, Bavaria, Baden and Württemberg, and tried to lure a larger one, Prussia, with the bait of Hanover, which France currently occupied. Prussia would not be drawn into action on either side, so Napoleon had to fight only two of the three major European land powers. As always he acted quickly.

While the Holy Roman Emperor had assigned Archduke Charles (1771–1847) 80,000 men for Venetia and the Tyrol, General Mack (1752–1828) in Germany had only 60,000. The Russians were marching to add their forces to Mack's, but Napoleon had no intention of allowing the rendezvous. While Mack trudged into Bavaria, moving slowly so that the Russians could catch up with him, the Army of Boulogne swept across the Rhine with astonishing speed and the army in Hanover hastened to link up with Napoleon in Württemberg. To confuse the enemy Napoleon then divided his forces into seven subdivisions, which fanned out into columns that converged close to Mack's forward base at Ulm on the Danube. On 20 October 1805, the day before Trafalgar, the astonished Mack and 50,000 men were obliged to surrender.

The campaign was not proceeding as the Third Coalition partners had expected. An army from Sicily forced the French to give up Naples and make a tactical retreat from southern Italy. But in the main theatre of war north of the Alps the Russians under Mikhail Kutuzov (1745–1813) were hampered by their strict instructions from the Tsar that the only non-Russian they should obey was the Holy Roman Emperor himself, or one of his archducal brothers. The only good general in the family, the Archduke Charles, was still *en route* from Italy back to Austria. As the French marched along the Danube towards Vienna, the Holy

Raffet's wash drawing of Napoleon the day before the battle of Austerlitz

Roman Emperor, perhaps hoping to prevent his capital being sacked, declared it an open city. The French entered unimpeded on 14 November.

In the campaign of 1805 Napoleon raised warfare to a new intensity. Hitherto military thinkers like Henri de la Tour d'Auvergne, vicomte de Turenne (1611–75), the finest of Louis XIV's marshals, had taken it as axiomatic that nobody could handle an army much larger than 50,000. Coming from what was then the most populous country in Europe, and with his well-disciplined army split into small, self-ordering units, Napoleon managed to fight with his normal rapid movement while manipulating an army of some 200,000 men.

After their systematic looting and requisitioning of supplies, including large amounts of armaments in the vicinity of Vienna, the members of the Grand Army, as historians know it, were tired. Napoleon had to pause but he could not afford to wait long. He must drive back the Russians before they produced yet more serfs for their peasant army, he must defeat the main Austrian army before the Archduke Charles arrived back from Italy, and he must strike before the Prussian king, now inclined to war, made up his mind to act. Napoleon moved into Bohemia.

On 23 October, the Russians under Kutuzov joined up with the Austrians under Archduke Ferdinand at Braunau on the River Inn. Though Napoleon tried to prevent it, Kutuzov and Ferdinand were then able to link up with another Russian army under Friedrich Wilhelm Buxhowden. Having found a convenient site near the village of Austerlitz, Napoleon hid 22,000 men detached from his main force while displaying the rest of his army of some 50,000 temptingly close to the joint Russo-Austrian army of some 90,000. He made himself appear still more vulnerable by ordering his generals to vacate the hilly ground known as the Pratzen Heights, so offering his enemies the added advantage of occupying the vantage point that commanded the site of the projected battlefield. On 1 December the allies occupied the heights.

The battle that began the following dawn has been regarded as Napoleon's masterpiece. The arrival of the 22,000 men that Napoleon had hidden away, led by Louis Davout (1770–1823), caused Buxhowden's Russians to beg urgently for reinforcement from their allies on the Pratzen Heights in the centre of the battlefield. Napoleon deliberately and progressively weakened his right wing, drawing ever more allied troops to attack it and convincing the allies that they would cut him off from a possible retreat to Vienna. Then, after checking that his left could hold, he released the cavalry under Murat to drive the Russian cavalry from where they had been guarding the approach to the Pratzen Heights. When Murat had driven most of the Russian cavalry away, Napoleon released infantry and gunners under Nicolas Soult (1769–1851) from the centre of the French line to scale the heights and cut the allies, already depleted by their attacks against his right wing, in two. Now in command of the centre, the French could drive the right wing of the allied army towards marshes called the Satschen Mere. By dusk, which came early at that time of year, his troops had reduced the allied armies to a shambles.

That evening Napoleon relaxed to the music of Luigi Boccherini in the nearby château of Austerlitz. Next day he told Joséphine just that he had won a battle but was feeling a bit tired. When he wrote to Joseph, however, he was gloating: *I routed the allied armies under the personal command of the Emperors of Russia and Germany ... The whole army covered itself with glory.*[24] While the Russians scuttled back to Poland, next day Francis, Emperor of a thousand-year Reich, asked for an interview with the Emperor of 366 days and sued for terms.

The treaty of Pressburg, signed the day after Christmas 1805, completed the process of dismantling the Holy Roman Empire. Austria had to concede Venice, Istria and Dalmatia to Napoleon's new kingdom of Italy and to pay an enormous indemnity; the Austrians ceded Swabia to Württemberg and the Tyrol to Bavaria; Murat, Napoleon's favourite cavalry leader and husband of his sister Caroline, became the first Grand Duke of Berg, and Berthier, his minister of war and favourite staff officer, became Prince of Neuchâtel. Napoleon reorganised most of Germany to suit himself. His allies the Electors of Württemberg and Bavaria were made kings and their lands, together with Hesse-Darmstadt and the smaller southern and western principalities, were merged into a new unit called the Confederation of the Rhine. Since the 17th century it had been French policy to find German allies who would defy the Habsburgs, the ruling dynasty of the Holy Roman Empire. Now France had redrawn the political map.

Austria had to adapt. In August 1806 Francis II, who since 1804 had been also the Emperor Francis I of Austria, renounced his title as Holy Roman Emperor. This incoherent institution, which dated back to the time of Charlemagne, was no more, but then the ruler most like Charlemagne was not a Habsburg, but a Bonaparte. As Napoleon was soon telling his uncle Fesch: *For the Pope I am Charlemagne.*[25]

Strangely it was at this moment that Prussia, the one kingdom in Germany that Napoleon did not control, decided to defy him. Since 1786, when Frederick the Great had died, Prussia had lived on the reputation that he had earned. His nephew and successor Frederick William II (1744–97), a cultivated man who loved the music of Mozart and Beethoven, made vast territorial gains in the east by absorbing large chunks of northern Poland, saw his troops fail to check the French revolutionary armies in 1793–5 and then felt it wise to abstain from any conflict in the west. After his death in 1797, his ineffective son Frederick William III (1770–1840) tried to ignore the threat posed by the conquests of the French armies until he had no allies left to support him. Napoleon was obsessed by the humiliating memory of Frederick the Great's rout of the French at Rossbach in 1757 and was determined to show that the Grand Army was more than adequate to the task of revenge.

Frederick William was cowed by Napoleon, who specified which bits of Prussia he wanted for his marshals and said that the country was to close its ports to British commerce and ally exclusively with France. In return France would give the King the electorate of Hanover (which belonged to the King of England).

Napoleon on the battlefield at Jena from a painting by Horace Vernet

Prussia accepted all these terms, then thought of seeking help from the English, who pointed out who owned Hanover. Frederick William turned to Russia, whose Tsar promised to help – but not now. Having dithered so long, the Prussians then made the mistake of acting impulsively.

On 29 August the King sent Napoleon an ultimatum: his troops must evacuate the Confederation of the Rhine or Prussia would go to war. As he had a whole army in southern Germany, Napoleon's response was swift. He marched into Saxony, where the bulk of the Prussian troops were camped, concentrated most of his troops on the River Saale and dispatched Davout to prevent the Prussians from retreating towards the River Elbe. On 14 October, Davout faced the main Prussian army at Auerstädt, while to the south at Jena Napoleon was confronted with a mere covering force. The remarkable speed and manoeuvrability of the French forces won both battles, but Davout's was the greater achievement, for the Prussian army under the old Duke of Brunswick and the King was more than double the size of his. For the Prussians Jena-Auerstädt was a catastrophe: the French managed to turn their enemy's retreat into a rout, pursuing their foe till they had taken 150,000 prisoners and overrun three-quarters of Prussian territory. Prussia had to cede lands between the Rhine and the Elbe rivers, so that it now owned little to the west of Prussia itself, and the King, refusing to accept Napoleon's terms, fled to Königsberg, modern Kaliningrad, in East Prussia, where Napoleon ignored him. Napoleon visited the palace of Sans-Souci in Potsdam and meditated at the tomb of his hero, Frederick the Great.

If he was to impose his will on the whole of central Europe, Napoleon's final task was to neutralise the threat from Russia. He regarded the Russian infantry, which was composed of serfs, as ill-educated and ill-equipped, the artillery as excellent and the Cossack cavalry as superb. He had to make sure that the greater flexibility, better weaponry and superior leadership of the Grand Army would win out.

He was briefly distracted. On his way east in the run-up to Christmas 1806, he visited Warsaw and there saw a girl he thought exceptionally beautiful. She was Maria Walewska (1786–1817), the 18-year-old wife of a Count aged 77 and mother of his child. It took several days, the persuasive powers of fervent Polish nationalists, among them her own husband, as well as the seductive technique of Napoleon, to convince her that it was her duty to become his lover. In the end she gave way, then found she was falling in love with him, so that the cold nights of January were passed in the enjoyment of an idyll such as Napoleon had not known since he first met Joséphine. This time he was frantic to prevent his wife from joining him and he had to write a series of letters to pretend that his concern for her impelled him to beg her not to join him: *I can't possibly allow any woman to undertake the journey here. The roads are too bad – unsafe, and muddy. Go back to Paris; be happy, be glad; perhaps I will come soon.*[26] About the same time he was assuring his new love: *Marie, my sweet Marie, my first thoughts are of you, my first desire is to see you again.*[27]

Sadly the Russian commander Bennigsen brought his enjoyment to an end when he began to move troops up in preparation for a spring offensive. Worse still, a confused courier let the Russians know the plan Napoleon had devised to lure them into a trap. When there was a major battle, in East Prussia, early in February 1807, it was therefore the French who were caught off balance. Marching into a blizzard, the reserves on which Napoleon was obliged to call could not see their targets and might have been decimated but for one of Murat's most daring cavalry charges to seize the Russian guns that had been doing all the damage. In the end only the arrival of the corps commanded by Michel Ney (1769–1815), saved the French from defeat. The Russians' withdrawal allowed Napoleon to claim some kind of victory, but he knew that, though he was left in control of the field of Eylau, he was left also with piles of dead and dying men. Napoleon remarked, *If all the kings on earth could see this sight, they would be less greedy for wars and conquests.*[28] Ney was more succinct. 'What a massacre,' he said, 'and without a result.'

Napoleon eventually recovered his poise. On 14 June at Friedland he ordered Marshal Lannes, who was outnumbered 45,000 to 17,000, to encourage the Russians to cross the River Alle, leaving them with few bridges over which they could retreat if they needed. Fighting stubbornly, Lannes was able to pin the Russians down near the bank until the mass of the French army could come from Eylau, where it was still stationed. When Lannes had been sufficiently reinforced to stop the Russians, his staff urged Napoleon to wait till the next day, when extra reinforcements would give him an overwhelming advantage. Napoleon did not agree. He had noticed that the Russians had their backs to a town and a winding river and that a lake cut their front in two. It was too good an opportunity to miss. There was another, more emotional reason why he should attack. Just as Austerlitz had occurred on the anniversary of his coronation, so Friedland would occur on the anniversary of Marengo. His superstitious belief in his star pressed him to fight immediately, though it was almost four o'clock in the afternoon. He was quickly proved right. Some Russians were driven into Friedland, which the French set alight, others were driven back towards the bridges, where in the crush hardly anyone could move. With his army shattered, the Tsar had no choice but to sue for peace.

The Emperor and the Tsar made peace at Tilsit on a pontoon in the River Niemen. They divided Europe between them, humiliating Prussia. Napoleon carved out the Kingdom of Westphalia from Prussia's western lands for his brother Jérôme – his brother Louis was already King of Netherlands – and from Prussia's eastern lands in Poland the Grand Duchy of Warsaw. (The rest of Poland remained in Russian hands.) Russia lost only the Ionian Islands in the Mediterranean.

French troops in Italy had meanwhile consolidated and expanded French rule there. Elise Bonaparte was already Duchess of Lucca, a city she did not think important enough, and she amassed other towns till she was Grand Duchess of Tuscany, nominally as wife to a nonentity called Felice Bacchiochi (1762–1841). Pauline meanwhile had struck gold by marrying Camillo Borghese (1775–1832), heir to a family fortune. She had been offered the tiny town of Guastalla in Emilia, which she sold to the kingdom of Italy. After Friedland, Napoleon made her husband governor-general of Turin.

In 1806 the French had marched into Rome, where Lucien, who had fallen out with his bossy brother, was sulking. Much papal territory had been taken already. The Holy See would lose the rest when the French took control of Rome in 1808, annexing it a year later. When the Pope excommunicated Napoleon in 1809, the French seized the Pontiff and held him in Savona. Lastly, the King of the Two Sicilies had been driven back to the one Sicily, the island, that the British navy could protect; the other half of the kingdom, on the mainland, became the domain of Joseph as King of Naples. Mainland Italy had been cut into three parts, all under French control: in the north west it was effectively an extension of imperial France; in the north east Napoleon himself ruled the Kingdom of Italy; and in the south Joseph ruled the Kingdom of Naples, to be succeeded, from 1808, by Napoleon's brother-in-law Joachim Murat.

By summer 1807, then, Napoleon dictated the political map of Europe from the borders of Spain to the borders of Russia, from southern Italy to the Baltic. Only Britain remained undefeated and inviolate. To change that would involve him in a new kind of fighting. As he declared, *I want to conquer the sea by the power of the land.*[29] His solution was to conduct economic warfare. Decrees at Berlin in December 1806 and in Milan a year later were meant to drive the British Isles into economic isolation. The continent would be closed to its trade. All British goods would be excluded from continental ports; all ships that had passed through British ports would be seized. The British retaliated by making laws insisting that all seaborne trade both with and within the continent, no matter whom it involved, must pass through British ports. They blockaded every continental port to enforce the law.

Napoleon's measures went hand in hand with an effort to stimulate trade on land, but in an age when roads were often impassable, no railways existed and there was no adequate way of moving freight except by water, his policy was premature. His regulations were disastrous for ports from Bordeaux to Danzig, which had traded either across the Atlantic or else directly with Britain and his desire to make the whole continent comply with his wishes caused resentment and stimulated smuggling from

St Petersburg to Marseille. Joséphine blithely went on ordering plants for her garden at Malmaison from George III's nurseries at Kew. A more serious act of defiance came from his brother Louis, who, though a foreign King of Holland, had learnt to speak Dutch and sympathised with Amsterdam's merchants. He contrived not to enforce the decrees.

To give cohesion to the lands whose fortunes he decided, Napoleon created a new class of imperial rulers, who were entirely loyal to him. He revived the French title of Marshal for his most eminent soldiers and gave them titles from far-off regions: Berthier, as already mentioned, became Prince of Neuchâtel in 1806 and Bernadotte, husband to Joseph's sister, had been Prince of Pontecorvo since 1805. In 1808 Davout (after an interval, since his victory had to be downplayed) became Duke of Auerstädt, Augereau, a veteran of the first Italian campaign, became Duke of Castiglione, Lannes, another veteran of Italy, became Duke of Montebello, and Massena became Duke of Rivoli. The marshals came from different social classes but they were made senators for life, given access to large incomes, encouraged to live expensively and to dress like peacocks. Success in war gave them the chance to add to their wealth by looting in a fashion that mimicked Napoleon's own behaviour.

Napoleon, knowing that he must also create and sustain a ruling class, became obsessed by the need for a meritocratic education system for its benefit. The Revolution had swept away the old clerical monopoly on schooling but few other than Marie-Jean Antoine Nicolas Caritat, sometime marquis de Condorcet (1743–96), had thought much about what to put in its place. Condorcet, the foremost mathematician of his age and a rationalist who believed that the advance of science was the key to human progress in civilization, had put forward a plan in 1792 for a system of state schools. Fellow members of the Legislative Assembly listened respectfully, ordered the printing of his plan and then did nothing to implement it. In 1794 to 1795, after the fall of Robespierre, the Thermidorians set up many institutions of higher learning and advanced skills: a Conservatory of Arts and Crafts, a School of Mines, three schools of medicine, veterinary schools, an Institute for Deaf-Mutes, a Bureau of Longitude (vital for sailors), a School of Oriental Languages, a Museum of French Monuments and, most famously, the Ecole Polytechnique, an institution to train engineers, and the Ecole Normale Supérieure, an institution to train teachers.

Only after Napoleon became Emperor, however, did the French government commit itself to a national system of education suited to the perceived needs of modern France. Napoleon was enough a child of the Revolution to think that such a system must be uniform. He was just as sure that the country should have the equivalent of a Minister of Education as he took for granted the existence of Ministers of the Interior, Finance and Defence.

He had already established the lycées, which he began setting up in 1802, as the first stage in secondary education. The lycée, the one Napoleonic educational institution to have endured, made a standard academic education available to the middle classes, offering a gateway to higher study. For students with special academic gifts competitive examinations became the normal route to specialist institutions like the schools of application – where pupils studied the arts of mining, artillery or building roads and bridges – or the Ecole Polytechnique. But, though entry was meritocratic, it was open only to those already in the meritocracy and so became self-perpetuating. The Polytechnique had been concerned with scientific research and been open to the poor, but from 1804–5 it charged fees and concentrated on just preparing engineers for the armed forces.

On 10 May 1806 Napoleon promulgated a law to provide a body to supervise all education: the University of France, based in Paris, which was described as 'a body charged exclusively with public teaching and education in the whole Empire ... [and meant] to direct political and moral opinions.'[30] For the post of Grand Master of the University Napoleon chose Louis de Fontanes (1757–1821), a conservative literary dabbler who instilled a Catholic ethos into the academies (geographical areas). These in turn had a hierarchy that reached down from the rector of each academy via inspectors to the principals of the lycées. The intention was to concentrate on the provision of tertiary as well as secondary levels of education, but at first French universities could only boast adequate faculties of law and medicine; in the arts and sciences there was rarely much progress beyond secondary levels.

What was not yet in place was an adequate system of primary schools to replace the old Church schools. Inevitably, many former members of religious orders eked out a living in later years by teaching, and it took more than one generation to provide enough teachers.

Even when away campaigning, Napoleon took time to think about the issues his government faced. While relaxing to the south of Eylau at the castle of Finkenstein, where he had been since 1 April 1807, he drafted a long, careful letter responding to suggestions for setting up a faculty of literature and history at the Collège de France. He argued against teaching literary skills at university on the grounds that any student should have learnt all he needed to know at secondary school. The teaching of history, and, for that matter, geography, on the other hand, he saw as vital. He imagined a syllabus ranging widely from the history of the church, law since Roman times and the art of war to the stories of individual countries. His idea of a humanities course was one that would enable a French soldier or diplomat to best serve his country.

The Napoleonic system 1808–11

Napoleon had created a new form of social organisation in France. In 1802 he had set up the Legion of Honour to reward faithful service in civilian or, more often, military occupations, in 1804 he created princes, in 1806 dukes and in 1808 counts, barons and chevaliers (knights). Decorations and titles bound men, and their families, to him. This did not mean that he was reverting to the old regime that had existed before 1789, for he made sure that all those he promoted could afford their status; none of his nobles would be impoverished members of a privileged caste. Others who had prominent places in the judiciary, the administration or legislative and consultative institutions were simply notables. They too had to be sufficiently rich. By establishing this plutocratic regime he would ensure that his idea of a modern society would endure.

His reformed French society would be a model for all Europe, but only if he mastered all Europe. In a series of remarkable campaigns from the autumn of 1805 to the summer of 1807 French armies had crushed the three other major continental European powers, Austria, Prussia and Russia. He had reorganised three European countries (Germany, Italy and Poland) in ways that suited France. In the past strong kings like Louis XIV had operated on the principle of divide and dominate, so that France had cultivated client states such as Bavaria or Florence (later Tuscany) which could be relied on to check traditional foes like Austria or Milan under Habsburg control. Napoleon had so reduced the influence of the two key Germanic states, Prussia and Austria, that they no longer counted as serious rivals. In Italy, there was no state to check France. Russia was now the only counterbalance to his power in central and eastern European affairs.

The third country Napoleon had reorganised, Poland, hemmed in by Russia, Prussia and Austria, had been a long-time client of France. Though neither Louis XV in 1772 nor the French Republic in 1793 and 1795 could stop Poland from being partitioned, the Poles retained a touching trust that the French would restore their country to its former greatness. After all, even before setting up the Grand Duchy of Warsaw, Napoleon was in love with his Polish mistress; and Napoleon did not find it hard to attract gallant Polish soldiers to fight for him in the Grand Army.

Now Napoleon turned his attention to the Iberian peninsula. Spain had joined the First Coalition against France in the early 1790s, which could be thought a gesture of solidarity with fellow monarchs, but switched allegiances when French troops reached the Ebro river and threatened Madrid. Alliance with France had certain disadvantages, for it meant that twice, off Cape St Vincent in 1797 and off Cape Trafalgar in 1805, the British had annihilated the Spanish fleet. In 1801 France had forced Spain to declare war on Portugal. The Spaniards took a border town, the royal favourite Manuel de Godoy picked some oranges – an action that gave the so-called war its nickname – and the Portuguese agreed to close their ports to the British (a decision the British accepted). Both Spain and Portugal were required to give France money to avoid being attacked.

Francisco Goya y Lucientes (1746–1828) was court painter of Charles IV before serving Joseph Bonaparte. Of anticlerical opinions, initially he was pro-French, but he later celebrated Madrid's resistance in 1808. In his series of pictures *The Disasters of War* he showed his horror at all the suffering caused by civil war.

By 1808, however, passive alliances or neutrality were not

Napoleon rests at his encampment the night before the French enter Madrid

enough for Napoleon. He sent troops to take over Portugal, the Portuguese royal family fled to its colony of Brazil, and French flags soon flew over Lisbon. He then demanded a meeting at Bayonne with the King of Spain, his heir Ferdinand, Prince of the Asturias (1784–1833), who was plotting to replace him, and Godoy. At the end of the meeting the whole royal family was forced into exile, Napoleon announced that his brother Joseph would become Spain's new King and on 2 May 1808 the people of Madrid rose in revolt.

In Portugal too resistance led to a revolt, which in this case was supported by a British army under a general named Arthur Wellesley (1769–1852), who had led British forces to victory in India. After his first victories at Vimiero (in Portugal) and Talavera (in Spain) he became better known as the Duke of Wellington. Before the end of the year Napoleon himself felt obliged to come to the peninsula, above all to make sure that his brother was secure in Madrid. He sent Soult and Ney to chase another British general, Sir John Moore (1761–1809), all the way to Corunna, where they were repulsed before most of the British escaped. Early in 1809

Napoleon left Spain for good, having failed to pacify either of the peninsular countries and leaving behind a series of conflicts, which none of the many marshals who fought there could resolve.

He had a more serious matter to cope with: a resurgent Austria. In one of Napoleon's typically dangerous miscalculations, he never thought that either Prussia or Austria would dare dispute the destiny he had allotted to them. Both, however, began to show that defeat could be a spur to change. In East Prussia, where the King was now based in the eastern city of Königsberg, able civil servants, among whom the key figure was Heinrich Stein (1757–1831), instituted a series of reforms. Stein, a Rhinelander who arrived at court on 30 September 1807, wanted the middle classes and peasants to be allowed to own land and the nobility to be allowed to go into trade. He insisted that those in high places should be able. Gerhard von Scharnhorst (1755–1813), a Hanoverian, was made head of the military cabinet attached to the ministry of war. By his heroic defence of the fortress of Colberg, August von Gneisenau (1760–1831), a Saxon, was one of the few Prussian soldiers who had enhanced his reputation in 1806. Together these two took over responsibility for turning the anti-quated Prussian army into a force that could cope with the French. Previously every company had been independent, now all of them became parts of a single national force.

Stein had brought the sick Prussian body politic back to health. When Prussian nobles, or junkers, worried by Stein's changes, passed on their anxieties to Napoleon, he forced Frederick William to dismiss his talented minister after only a year's service and exile him from Prussia and the Confederation of the Rhine. Prussia therefore remained as Napoleon wanted it, a cumbersome, eastern European state. But the modernising of its army was underway and young intellectuals, of whom Germany with its many universities sported an inordinate number, had begun to think that Prussia was the state that could unite the German *Volk* against France.

A similar process occurred in Austria. Again, the upper classes resisted, so that Chancellor Johann Philipp von Stadion (1763–1824) opted for modest reforms like setting up manufacturing firms, establishing schools and building roads. The one attempt at being radical was left to the ablest royal general, Archduke Charles. He was made generalissimo and, despite a shortage of money, copied the French corps system, making units of the army into complete miniature armies (a system Napoleon had used with devastating effect in the march on Ulm). The Archduke also improved drill and brought the artillery up to date. If he had not found a way to counteract Napoleonic warfare, he had at least learned how to fight as if he were a pupil of Napoleon.

Meanwhile, as with Prussia, the intellectuals had been working out a distinctive role for Austria, not so much in Germany, since almost all Austrian dominions lay outside that country, as in Europe, since its imperial past gave Austria a special function as defender of Christian or at least Catholic civilization.

With the French tied down in Spain, the war party in Vienna saw an opportunity to get back at Napoleon. The Austrians hoped for military help from Russia and financial help from Britain, but neither country would promise assistance. Like the Prussians in 1806, they decided to declare war, against the Archduke Charles's wishes, without being able to rely on any committed friends. They then made the additional mistake of attacking on three fronts, in Poland, Italy and Bavaria. They also underestimated Napoleon's ability to raise troops, partly by increasing the numbers of French conscripts, but also by leaning on his nominal allies. The Grand Army was now polyglot, with few elite, French-speaking units other than the Guard, which was soon withdrawn from Spain.

Reckoning correctly that he must attack the most talented general, Archduke Charles in Germany, instead of Archduke John (1782–1859) in Italy or Archduke Ferdinand (1781–1850) in Poland, Napoleon drove the Austrians back along the Danube out of Vienna. But he lost touch with the main body of the Austrians and at Aspern Archduke Charles suddenly attacked with a larger force and drove the French back (what Napoleon called a with-drawal). Forced to regroup, he took time to gain a massive supe-riority in numbers by recalling troops from Spain, built strong bridges over the Danube, and was cheered by the news that the Army of Italy had defeated Archduke John. Then and then only was he ready to turn on Archduke Charles and pulverise him at Wagram on 5 to 6 July. It was to be his last major victory. It caused Archduke Charles to resign and gave Napoleon his one last chance to impose tough terms on another Emperor.

While lingering at Schönbrunn, the Habsburg palace outside Vienna, he resumed his affair with Maria Walewska and made her pregnant. He rejoiced that 'his' Poles had helped in another way by beating Archduke Ferdinand. He then set about disman-tling Austria. It had to give up its southern possessions, Carinthia, Carniola and Croatia, to France, Salzburg and the upper valley of the Inn to Bavaria, southern Poland to the Grand Duchy of Warsaw and a piece of Poland to Russia. There was resistance in the Tyrol but it quickly collapsed.

Never had Napoleon's hold over central Europe seemed so strong. But, though he had won a battle and dictated a peace, he no longer won over hearts and minds. In Vienna an 18-year-old Saxon named Friedrich Staps tried to stab him but was quickly overpowered. Anxious to appear merciful, Napoleon arranged to interview the young man. Staps repeatedly told him that he regretted only his failure, so that Napoleon felt obliged to have him executed. Napoleon was bewildered that his magnetism no longer drew the young towards him.

He still did not feel secure. He was head of a dynasty, but his only possible male heirs would be the sons of his brother Louis. He needed a son of his own and the mother must come from what he thought was his class. As he went back to France, he was already

Maria Walewska

sure that he must divorce Joséphine. Since 1807 his advisers had talked about an impending divorce but every time the matter was raised Joséphine had used her charm to survive. After the treaty of Schönbrunn Napoleon made up his mind that his imperial power must be perpetuated in a son, and a legitimate one. (When his son Alexandre was duly born in Poland to Maria Walewska, he was given the surname of her husband, not Bonaparte.) During tearful scenes at Fontainebleau in the last week of October Napoleon completed the first stage of his plan by making clear to Joséphine that she must go; and in December they were divorced. The Beauharnais stepchildren were crestfallen, the Bonaparte sisters exultant and it took curt words from Napoleon to put them in

Napoleon bids farewell to Joséphine after announcing his intention to
divorce her

their place. His behaviour was dynastic rather than tribal; and he
did not care much for his tribe.

He would have liked to marry a Romanov, but the Tsar, whom

he had cultivated assiduously, had been cool during their Erfurt meeting in 1808, was ambiguous during the Austrian campaign until Napoleon was victorious and stalled when Napoleon asked for the hand of the Tsar's sister the Grand Duchess Anna (at 16 she was too young). Napoleon turned to the Habsburgs. The new Austrian foreign minister Count Klemens Wenzel von Metternich (1773–1859) told his master it was prudent to give way. They worried only that the marriage might not be valid. Napoleon's relations with the Pope had deteriorated so far that he was now an excommunicate. When the Archbishop of Vienna raised doubts about Napoleon's freedom to marry, Cardinal Fesch was on hand to maintain that since Napoleon's religious marriage of 1804 had been irregular in form (there were no witnesses) and in intention (Napoleon had been forced into it), it was invalid. With Habsburg consciences soothed, the Archduchess

On seeing the King of Rome's portrait, Napoleon called his son *the most beautiful child in France.*[31] He later said, *I would rather his throat was slit than see him brought up in Vienna as an Austrian prince.*[32] But François-Charles-Napoléon was taken there (1814) and there he died (1832).

Marie-Louise was told she must do her duty and was delighted to find that, when she did it, she enjoyed the experience. By conceiving and bearing a son, Napoleon, King of Rome (1811–32), she made her husband's happiness seem complete.

Napoleon suffered from the sense of obligation that bound him to his siblings. As a good Corsican he was obliged to provide for them. He had made almost all not just princes and princesses but, wherever possible, grand dukes or duchesses, sometimes even kings. Only Lucien, who resented his brother and was disliked in return, had lost out, though he was compensated when the Pope, to whom he had lent money, made him Prince of Canino. Sadly, most of the Bonapartes and their spouses were incompetent. Unlike hereditary rulers, they had not been brought up to rule and, unlike their brother or brother-in-law, they did not have a natural ability to rule.

Joseph, to whom Napoleon felt obliged to give more than the others out of some lingering respect for his status as older brother, was lazy, shrewd in money matters, cultivated and conciliatory. He was good at encouraging the opera and the theatre in Naples or Madrid and went down well with anyone who disliked ancient feudal ways or regarded the influence of the clergy as excessive, but he could not begin to understand the fanatical hatred that his policies provoked among the devout, illiterate peasants of remoter regions. Outside towns the French never had any support and in Madrid the brutal suppression of the revolt of 2 May 1808 left a permanent sense of resentment against the foreign intruders.

In Spain, the *afrancesados*, the Francophile nobles and middle classes who stood for enlightened reform, had welcomed the French at first. But the French habit of living off the country when on campaign made French soldiers still more unpopular than those other foreign soldiers, the British, whom Wellington was careful to provision with long lines of supplies. Especially in hilly or mountainous land, it was only too easy to ambush a stray French soldier or even a small French force. Attacking the hated foreigners became a national occupation, so any peasant, even a peasant woman, even a village priest could not be trusted. The attacks were so frequent and so successful that the Spanish word for a little war, a *guerrilla*, became familiar all over Europe. Joseph's liberal intentions could not disguise the fact that the French were successful chiefly in uniting previously hostile factions against the foreign occupier.

In certain ways the brother who made the best ruler was Louis. Though a nagging husband whose paranoia eventually pushed his beautiful wife, Hortense de Beauharnais, into infidelity, he set out to be a model king. He behaved like a bourgeois monarch with the pompous assertiveness of a wealthy businessman. He learned Dutch, was involved in the establishment of a national art gallery in Amsterdam, the nucleus of the future Rijkmusuem, had a national archive formed in The Hague, and brought to a conclusion the process of codifying Dutch law. In retirement he was to write, 'In Holland the interests, cares and public affairs occupied me entirely.'[33] As far as his elder brother was concerned, that was the trouble. When 'Koning Lodewijk' protested to his brother against the enforcement of the Continental System, Napoleon, who had regarded Louis as his protégé, was furious. In 1810 he dismissed him.

Napoleon's baby brother Jérôme and his brother-in-law Murat were liabilities because they were fools. Jérôme could not remember when the family had been poor. As far as he was concerned, the luck of the Bonapartes meant that he should be indulged. After an unfortunate marriage to an American that Napoleon, though not the Pope, refused to acknowledge, his brother married him off to Princess Catherine of Württemberg (1782–1835). As King of Westphalia, he was given charge of a number of small principalities artificially welded together. He abolished traces of feudalism but retained the right to act like a feudal lord in matters of sexual politics, for he made a habit of sleeping with his wife's ladies-in-waiting. He pointedly tolerated Jews and did not distinguish between commoners and noblemen, while lavishing enormous sums on his own perfumes and clothes.

Despite his physical courage and success as leader of Napoleon's cavalry, Murat, the Grand Duke of Berg before taking over from Joseph as King of Naples, had no ability to lead. He was left in no doubt that his chief duty was to obey. *Remember I have made you king only for my system*, Napoleon told him.[34] In Berg he was made to raise cash for the Grand Army. In Naples Joseph had abolished feudal courts. Joachim I, as Murat was styled, got rid of internal customs, reduced interest rates, improved roads and bridges. He did not attempt to be strict about excluding British goods, but then it was impossible to control what went on in the distant regions of the kingdom, a natural focus for brigands and smugglers.

Beyond the inner circle of family members lay an outer circle of lesser family members, marshals and ministers. His sister Elise and her husband were placed in charge of a number of Italian cities that in the end added up to Etruria, the classical name for Tuscany. Pauline's Borghese husband was allotted Piedmont and Liguria. Auguste Marmont (1774–1852), a marshal who had been a friend almost since Toulon days, was given control of Illyria, modern Croatia.

The most loyal and competent of all was Napoleon's stepson, Eugène de Beauharnais, Viceroy of Italy from 1806. 'Italy', cobbled together like most of Napoleon's political creations, extended from Lombardy and Venetia in the north (the Trentino, further north, was added after the Austrian campaign of 1809) to the Marches halfway down the Adriatic coast. As Napoleon was its king, it had to be the model for all the French-occupied territories. His Italy had its police chief, its administrators of canals and causeways, of health, of poor relief and of education. There was a school for girls in Milan, a school of bridges and roads, a veterinary school, a music conservatory and three academies of art. The Civil Code was introduced and with it civil marriage, divorce and a new system of inheritance. Church affairs were regulated according to the principles of the Concordat; the imperial catechism, which made disobedience to Napoleon a mortal sin, was taught in schools and churches; the number of seminaries was reduced and convents suppressed. A few aristocrats found Eugène's court attractive, but the enthusiasts for Napoleon's regime were men from the middle classes, who liked working as French civil servants. No other parts of Napoleon's Europe were so readily absorbed into Napoleon's Grand Empire as the eastern and western sides of the peninsula north of the kingdom of Naples.

Napoleon never created a united Europe, partly because he never managed much of Europe for more than a few years. But some of his policies have had lasting effects. If for up to 200 years much of Europe has had the institution of civil marriage and divided inherited property into equal shares, conceded emancipation to the Jews and toleration to Protestant and Catholic minorities, operated standard routines of administration, used the metric system and driven on the right, that is because of Napoleon. Napoleon also envisaged a common continental market in trade. But his dictatorial cast of mind and his determination to subordinate the needs of subject territories to the needs of France as he saw them vitiated his achievement. It is perhaps a fitting irony that the nation that ultimately gained most from the centralising of the European economy, along with the roads, the bridges and the postal service that he planned, turned out to be Germany.

Napoleon had reduced the number of principalities and set up the Confederation of the Rhine. Though the Confederation partly owed its existence to Napoleon's demand for troops, as was clear when the members promised him 63,000 men, he had also established the idea of unifying Germany; after he was gone, Germany was linked together in a new confederation under the presidency of Austria in place of France. This German confederation was not a new version of the Holy Roman Empire, but a body of small sovereign states that developed a habit of co-operation; and, when in 1834 a customs union or *Zollverein* joined many of the north German states to the economic fortunes of Prussia, that became a stage on the route towards eventual German unification under Prussia in 1866 and 1871.

To Poles Napoleon might have seemed spontaneously generous when he created the Grand Duchy of Warsaw out of Prussian Poland; and some Polish nationalists imagined they discerned a natural sympathy with their cause after he had taken a Polish mistress and she had given him a son. And yet, though one of his marshals was the Pole Prince Joseph Poniatowski (1763–1813), he used his Polish allies the way he used his German allies – as a means of feeding the Grand Army's incessant hunger for recruits. The Polish Legions, as they were called, may have worn distinctive Polish uniform, but they were never used to fight for Polish independence. They were routed by the Russians in Italy in 1799, fell at Marengo in 1800 and at Hohenlinden in 1801. The French framed the constitution of the Grand Duchy and Napoleon appointed as Grand Duke Frederick Augustus (1750–1827), the first King of Saxony, whose family had given three kings to Poland in the previous century. In 1808 the Polish Chevaux Légers won glory when they rode to capture the cannons at the gates of Madrid.

The first time that Poles could identify with Napoleon's ambitions was 1809, when Poniatowski outmanoeuvred the Austrian Archduke Ferdinand in Poland itself; and after Napoleon's victory at Wagram the Grand Duchy was appropriately rewarded when it acquired Austria's Polish possessions of Cracow and West Galicia. Only in 1812, however, did the Poles feel enthusiastically pro-French, as their regiments took part in the attack on Russia which Napoleon called the Polish war; and any hopes that the Poles may have had for a Polish future went down as Poniatowski, mortally wounded, drowned in the waters of the River Elster in 1813, fighting to the last for a French Emperor who was powerless against the overwhelming force of the Germans and Russians, the two countries that had dismembered Poland in the unhappy 18th century, and would dismember it again, first in 1815 then in 1939.

As late as 1811 the French Empire seemed almost everywhere

indomitable. The exception was the Iberian peninsula, where in Portugal and later in Spain French troops were finding it harder to pin the countryside down. Wellington's troops were elusive, never taking on superior forces and retreating to Portugal, where he could rely on the navy. Whenever a battle seemed to him inevitable or opportune, Wellington had a knack of winning the encounter. He showed his mastery of defensive warfare when he prevented one of the best of Napoleon's marshals, Massena, from retaking Lisbon by massing his troops behind the impregnable Lines of Torres Vedras; and with still more skill he prevented French generals from combining against him. Meanwhile Spanish irregulars, with local knowledge, proved to be deadly enemies, able to cut communications almost at will, so that it was said it would take 400 men to deliver a letter from Paris to Madrid or from Madrid to Paris.

The trade warfare Napoleon waged against the English was intermittently successful. Britain's economy and therefore its government's finances relied on trade. At first it seemed as if Napoleon had done little to harm the quantity of Britain's exports, as the value of the goods involved went up steadily from £41 million in 1805 to over £50 million in 1809; at the same time the value of colonial goods that were re-exported rose from about £10 million in 1805 to almost £16 million in 1809. It is even true that the proportion of British goods exported to continental countries grew, from 38 per cent in 1805, to 42 per cent in 1810. But the blockade caused more difficulties than these figures indicate. Britain could not go on selling more and more goods to South America, as their clients there found it hard to pay for them. In North America, Britain's relations with the United States, which objected to British searches of neutral shipping, deteriorated steadily; and enforcing the retaliatory British blockade of continental ports put a strain on British resources.

In 1809 Britain turned down Austria's request for subsidies

in its battle against Napoleon. The British government was too committed to the peripheral fight in the Iberian peninsula to do much to help defeat Napoleon in the more crucial battle for the control of central Europe. And then in 1811 the crisis came. Partly because of the economic cycle, there was a dramatic fall in exports everywhere. The value of the pound had been falling for some years and in 1811 Britain could not obtain the gold bullion to shore up its reserves. Firms went bankrupt, there were problems caused not so much from glut, as Napoleon wanted, as from shortage. It was hard to get wool from Germany, silk from Italy, timber from Scandinavia, wheat from the German Baltic ports.

Industrial unrest began, which famously reached its height in 1812, as the mysterious 'King' Ned Ludd incited fellow workers to take revenge on the modern machines that were blamed for increasing unemployment. French corsairs, of whom the most celebrated was Robert Surcouf (1773–1827) from St Malo, damaged British trade by seizing British merchant vessels at a rate of about 600 a year in 1807–10 and Britain compounded its troubles by falling out with one of its most important trading partners, when in 1812 it drifted into war with the United States. Luckily for Britain, Napoleon was about to make an even bigger mistake.

Decline and first fall 1812–14

After his meeting with Alexander I in 1807 Napoleon was convinced that he had found an admirer. The young Tsar, famous for his own charm, was susceptible to charm in others; and Napoleon could turn on the charm whenever he found it useful. Alexander was delighted to hear Napoleon imply at one stage that Russians should be installed in Constantinople, as the idea answered to his longings as a devout Orthodox Christian to reverse the catastrophe of 1453, when the infidel Turks had taken over the spiritual heart of eastern Christianity, but he never developed a coherent policy to retake the Turkish capital. Napoleon went so far as to suggest that from Constantinople Russia and its allies should march on the Euphrates, threatening the route to India, to make Britain tremble. This was the heady language that could stir the Tsar's sympathy; and yet little by little the two men fell out of love.

When they met again at Erfurt in 1808, Napoleon found his friend more self-possessed and distant. He did not know that his own Foreign Minister, Talleyrand, had told Alexander that it was up to Russia to save Europe from Napoleon. Alexander already sensed that his own interests were antithetical to Napoleon's, for why must the French, unchallenged, dictate the affairs of central Europe? When a Russian army captured Moldavia and Wallachia on the Black Sea, Napoleon did not encourage the Tsar to take any more Turkish land. When Napoleon asked him for the hand of his younger sister the Grand Duchess Anna, Alexander did not reject him, but he also did not say he approved. He annoyed Napoleon by proposing that any signs of Polish identity, even in a crest, a flag or a uniform should be forbidden in Napoleon's Grand Duchy of Warsaw.

The Tsar's undertaking to support the continental ban on trade with Britain caused Russia hardship, so in 1810 Alexander reopened Russian ports to American ships (which could deliver British goods), relaxed his border controls on British exports and imposed heavy tariffs on French goods. Soon British goods, which got into Germany willy-nilly through the north German Baltic or Hanseatic ports, were flooding overland into Russia. Napoleon retaliated by annexing independent ports in the Baltic and outraged the Tsar by grabbing the Duchy of Oldenburg, whose heir was the husband of Alexander's sister Catherine, and then offering no compensation for his action.

Diplomatically Napoleon's conversations with the Tsar at Erfurt were not a success, but he enjoyed discussing classical drama with 'Monsieur Goeth' (Johann Wolfgang Goethe, 1749–1832). *You must write 'The Death of Caesar',* said Napoleon. *In this tragedy you must show the world how Caesar could have made mankind happy.* [35]

In 1811 Napoleon thought that the Tsar was set on confrontation, since he saw his own policy as essentially pacific. He merely wanted Alexander to be a friend, whereas Alexander wanted to trade with the British, extend his control over the Poles and eat further into Turkish territory on the Black Sea. Napoleon would not countenance another land power equal to his own and he convinced himself first that if Russia would not bend, it must be made to bend, and, secondly that if Russia was forced to bend, it would break.

His new Grand Army would be irresistible. To support the French core of troops he called on his German allies, led by Prussia and Austria, supplemented by Italian, Spanish, Portuguese, Belgian, Dutch, Swiss, German and Polish soldiers subject to his family or to other puppet rulers. He named the anticipated conflict the Polish war but he did not mean to fight a merely local conflict: he was heading a confederation of civilised Europeans against the barbarian hordes that threatened them all. From 25 June 1812, resplendent in uniforms of many colours and types, this huge array of around 450,000 troops moved steadily across the River Niemen into Russian territory. For the first time in his career Napoleon's army far outnumbered that of his enemy. No previous commander had ever had charge of such a colossal force. An epic encounter lay ahead, which would be surpassed only by the war of 1941–5.

Napoleon's efforts at reaching a truce with Britain had failed and in Spain Britain was well on the way to winning the sideshow struggle, doubtless helped by Napoleon's persistence in leaving that little war to his subordinates. The Russians, who expected they could not defeat the Grand Army in set battles, had taken note of the guerrilla tactics favoured by the native Spaniards. And while Napoleon had failed to make the peace that he needed, the Russians had eliminated two possible old enemies by coming to terms. They signed an accord with the Turkish Sultan and they secured the benevolent agreement of Sweden that, in return for an alliance, Russia would help Sweden take Norway from Napoleon's ally Denmark. Two traditional friends of France were rendered useless. France would have to rely on those who had been intimidated into being friends.

Almost from the beginning, Napoleon found he was fighting a war like no other that he had fought. The textbooks he had studied had advised him to live off the land, but he was entering a country of few people, hardly any fields, mean arable plots, not much livestock, poor communications and vast distances between towns. He had made himself an expert on mountain warfare, but now he found himself in a landscape where plains stretched to the distant horizon. With cover hard to find, there was no respite from the pitiless midsummer sun and few opportunities for springing an ambush. His cavalry could chase the Russian cavalry, but not fast enough to catch them; the celebrated Cossack horsemen were endlessly elusive. It did not seem to matter whether Napoleon had covered 100 miles or 500. He still could not bring the main Russian armies to bay. His lines of communication grew longer and longer and it became harder to transport food, clothing and ammunition or to bring up reinforcements. The troops grew tired, dirty, dishevelled and demoralised. Men began to desert in large numbers.

It was not much easier for the Russians. Their officers were aristocrats longing for a fight, the strategy of disengagement they were drifting into looked like cowardice, and as one after another Vilna, Minsk, Vitebsk and Smolensk fell to the French, the Tsar seemed insecure on his throne. He felt obliged to sack his commander, Mikhail Barclay de Tolly (1761–1818), and to recall the aged Kutuzov, whom he considered slovenly, chaotic and immoral. At last, as the French neared Moscow, the Russians made a stand. At Borodino the Russians lost up to 45,000 men, probably half their effective army, while the French lost only 10 to 20 per cent of each unit, but in heroic charges led by Ney or Murat they also lost virtually all their cavalry. On 14 September the invaders saw Moscow lying down below them. Kutuzov once more retreated, ignominiously deserting the old capital, as many of his compatriots saw it. The Grand Army, massively depleted by disease, injury and desertion, had reached its goal. The Tsar, even if safe far away in the capital, St Petersburg, would have to surrender.

Alexander did not make peace. Instead, the Russians started a fire in Moscow that destroyed many of the wooden buildings characteristic of the city. Napoleon's soldiers looted freely. Still he waited. Men were camping in the charred ruins, scavenging for food, already clutching round them whatever furs they had commandeered. Murat sent a messenger to Napoleon to say that

Napoleon's army enters a burning Moscow

the state of the cavalry alarmed him. Napoleon was sanguine. The troops, like him, were resting. Not till 13 October, when the city was covered in the first fine sprinkling of snow, did he concede that he would have to leave, having failed either to take the capital or carry out his basic war aim of annihilating the enemy army. On 18 October, after Kutuzov had surprised and defeated a section of the Grand Army under Murat in a skirmish, Napoleon finally realised that he must make haste. With about 100,000 men, less than a quarter of the number he had had in June, many of them sick and wounded, weighed down by what they had seized, short of nourishment, and encumbered by guns that were hard to drag across mud or ice, he ordered a withdrawal.

No episode in Napoleon's career has become so familiar as the tale of that retreat. Speed had always been his element. Now it was the Russians who could be quick. Time and again the French seemed to have been caught, at Malojaroslavetz on 24 October, at Viazma on 4 November, and, on potentially the most dangerous

The French army in retreat from Moscow from a drawing by Faber du Faur

occasion, at Borisov on the River Berezina on 25 November. On 18 November he told the minister for foreign affairs, *our position has grown worse. Almost all our horses – 30,000 of them – have perished as a result of the cold – 16 degrees of frost.*[36] And yet every time Napoleon and the marshals and the flower of the army escaped. The crossing of the River Berezina was particularly perilous. The main bridge at Borisov was down and the route to the north lay through impossible terrain, so Napoleon decided the only course possible was to feign a move to the south, hurry up north to a nearly fordable section of the river, have one new bridge under construction through the night and ready by noon and a second, stronger bridge ready by four in the afternoon. He sent most of the men across the first and the guns and any heavy equipment across the second. Not everyone got over: some fell in and were frozen solid; perhaps 9,000 were killed and 7,000 taken prisoner. But the crossing of the Berezina was a magnificent achievement, a surer sign of Napoleon's military genius than the numerous misjudgements that had wrecked the conduct of the campaign.

Napoleon had been with the army for the whole campaign and was personally in charge of crossing the Berezina, but on 5 December he decided it was politically necessary for him to take a fast carriage to Paris. On 22 October General Claude François de Malet had escaped from the private mental institution to which he had been confined and announced that Napoleon had died in Russia and that he was taking over the government. He contrived to arrest the Minister of Police and was only doubted after he had shot the Governor of Paris dead. His fellow conspirators were rounded up and executed. Napoleon sent word ahead that there had been some difficulties in Russia, though his army had never once been defeated, and, as for himself, the health of the Emperor was good. Once back he organised a series of court balls and lavish entertainments.

The Russian campaign was in some ways a curious expedition. Napoleon had not behaved in a way that his enemies might have expected. He had chased his foes without ever luring them to confront him when they did not want to. Once his enemies had eventually adopted a strategy of persistent withdrawal, Napoleon had no new plan. He had lost his remarkable ability to improvise. He did not go for the modern capital, St Petersburg, but for the ancient capital, Moscow. As he therefore never threatened the government directly, he could not impose his will on Alexander. He found out to his surprise that the capture of Moscow was not fatal to the Russian cause; and, having achieved no diplomatic success, he had to face military failure. He persuaded himself that only the weather had beaten him, but in failing to crush the Russians he raised Russian prestige to a new height. The Tsar whom five years ago Napoleon had flattered with his friendship at Tilsit was now the man who had saved the continent from French domination, the guarantor of a better, freer future. For a time Alexander could do no wrong, until it became apparent that his own position was tied into the preservation of a servile past.

Napoleon did not wish to accept that he could no longer decide the fate of nations. At the end of the month he wrote a charming, conciliatory letter to Pius VII, who was under house arrest at

Fontainebleau, to enquire after the Pope's health. Napoleon used his pen to woo any friend he could find and to keep others in their proper place. He soon reassured the King of Denmark that the Russians' accounts of his campaign were entirely untrue, rounded on Murat, to whose care he had entrusted the army, for leaving the army in the lurch, and set about raising a new army, this time composed mainly of Frenchmen. He knew he would have to face the victorious Russians again – they were following the advice of Stein, the reformer of Prussian administration whom Napoleon had had dismissed – and soon he heard that Prussia's craven king had changed sides. His best idea was to keep on good terms with Austria. In May he was counselling the Emperor Francis, *Do not throw away the fruit of three years' friendship*.[37] On 4 June he agreed to an armistice with Austria and on 26 June he had nine hours of discussion in Dresden, the capital of Saxony, with the Austrian Foreign Minister, Metternich. Metternich offered him peace on terms. Austria wanted its territories back, Prussia wanted the Confederation of the Rhine dissolved, Russia the same fate for the Grand Duchy of Warsaw.

Metternich, Napoleon understood, had made himself the spokesman of old Europe. In the name of his own, new Europe, Napoleon blurted out that, whereas hereditary rulers could be beaten many times and still recover, he had to be beaten only once and he was lost. Besides, he had recently had the better of two battles in Saxony: on 2 May, at the battle of Lützen, he had beaten the Russians; on 20–21 May, at Bautzen, he had beaten the three allies. He was not prepared to give up. Before they parted, Metternich told Napoleon that he had had his last opportunity for peace. That evening Napoleon learnt that his brother Joseph had just lost the battle of Vittoria in northern Spain. He agreed to extend his armistice till 10 August and to negotiate with his rivals at a conference in Prague in early August. Neither he nor they, however, believed that peace would come from the talks, and they were right. Having failed to conquer Russia and so to control eastern Europe, Napoleon was now trying to master Germany and so to control central Europe. If he were to lose there, he would be driven back to the fastness of France and the inner ring of its immediate neighbours. Being Napoleon, he was determined to win a decisive battle. The day after the end of the armistice, Austria declared war.

The outcome of the conflict would be affected by a new development: three experts on Napoleonic warfare had committed themselves to his opponents. Jean-Baptiste Bernadotte, married to Joseph's sister-in-law, Napoleon's first love Désirée, had been Minister of War in 1799 and was thought too much of a Jacobin to be invited to join the conspiracy of Brumaire. All the same, he became a Marshal in 1804. In 1810 the Swedes, desperate to find an heir for their childless king, had looked for help to their traditional friend, France, and invited Bernadotte to become their Crown Prince, with the hereditary right of succession. Little though he liked Bernadotte, Napoleon agreed, as he hoped thereby to weaken England's position in the Baltic, whose timber and pitch were so vital for its naval supplies. In 1812, however, well before the French defeat in Russia, Bernadotte had swapped sides; and it was as an ally of Russia that he was now invited to lead a Swedish army against his old rival.

Another soldier, Moreau, who had been implicated in the royalist plot of 1803, was living in exile in the USA. He returned to Europe and came to allied headquarters to act as adviser. He warned the Tsar that anyone who fought Napoleon was liable to be defeated, so his enemies should avoid him and attack his subordinates. Only then should they turn on him, and never give up.

The third expert was more of a theoretician. Antoine-Henri Jomini (1779–1869) was a Swiss who had served in the French army as aide-de-camp to Ney. He achieved fame as a military historian by publishing an account of the campaigns of Frederick the Great just before Napoleon attacked Prussia. Napoleon was so impressed that he invited Jomini to join his staff. He was with Napoleon at Jena in 1806 and at Eylau in 1807 and with Ney in Spain in 1808 but he was offered a Russian commission when Russia was France's ally and for some time held commissions in both armies with the agreement of both sovereigns. In the armistice of the summer of 1813, however, feeling slighted by Berthier, Napoleon's chief of staff, he joined the Russians definitively. Eventually he would write the standard account of Napoleon's style of fighting.

When the conflict began, the advice of all three men would prove invaluable. While the Austrians in Bohemia under Prince Karl Schwarzenberg (1771–1820) attacked from the south and the Prussians in Silesia under Gebhard von Blücher (1742–1819) attacked from the centre, the Swedes under their new Crown Prince, Bernadotte, attacked from the north, ensuring that Napoleon was forced to face armies from all sides. Napoleon was soon up to his old tricks, outmanoeuvring the Army of Bohemia at the battle of Dresden on 26–27 August just after other French armies had been defeated. Though Moreau was already dead, killed at Dresden, Blücher took his advice to avoid direct confrontations with Napoleon. In the end, after many manoeuvres and inconclusive battles, Napoleon failed to prevent the allies from concentrating their overwhelming strength against him, about 300,000 men to his 160,000. In the ensuing battle just outside Leipzig, the French were too tired and too weak to use their celebrated mobility to strike at first one part of the enemy's forces and then another. In a battle that lasted from 16 to 19 October, sheer force of numbers eventually overwhelmed them. Napoleon's initial assault soon lost its élan and for the next two days he tried in vain to extricate himself. Some 38,000 of Napoleon's soldiers were killed and another 30,000 taken prisoner.

The battle of Leipzig became the first major engagement that Napoleon lost. It is justly known as the 'Battle of the Nations', as it involved Russians, Austrians, Prussians, Swedes, and Poles besides Frenchmen, Italians and Germans from Saxony, Bavaria, Baden, Württemberg, Hesse and Westphalia. Napoleon may have thought that the many peoples who took part showed how international was his Empire, how European his cause. But just as the Russians had thought of the 1812 campaign as the great patriotic war, so the Germans would look back on the campaign of 1813 as the war of liberation. Napoleon's ambition to subordinate other nations to his will had provoked a nationalistic reaction.

Previously, all civilised aristocrats anywhere prided themselves on their ability to speak French, to mimic the splendours of Versailles, to adopt French fashions in costume and cuisine. Now Russian and German princes, dukes and counts took to learning their native tongues to talk to their own people. Russians turned to their ancient icons, while Germans became interested in their folk tales and the history of their language; and one painter, Caspar David Friedrich (1774–1840), invented a form of painting that was Lutheran and Germanic in its meaning, where solitary souls found God in Germanic forests or on Germanic mountain-tops or looking out to a northern sea.

Napoleon liked to think he was practical and so he withdrew from Germany, but he too thought in visionary terms – he believed if not in God, then in his star. When Metternich, speaking in the name of the victors, offered him France's natural borders on the Rhine, the Pyrenees and the Alps, while insisting that a Bourbon should be king of Spain and the northern Netherlands should be independent, Napoleon would not accept. Metternich, fearful of Russia, wished to keep France strong. Napoleon, unwilling to be anyone's equal, wished to keep France dominant. He left the allies no choice but to invade France itself.

The battles fought in 1814 on French soil were probably some of the most brilliant of Napoleon's career and certainly some of the most futile. Time and time again he showed that he could drive the Prussians back there, the Russians and Austrians back somewhere else. What he could not do was to deflect them from marching on Paris. He beat Blücher where he begun his studies of war, at Brienne, beat him three more times and also got the better of Schwarzenberg once. Then he thought he might accept Metternich's offer of settlement. But his gesture of conciliation had come too late, for at Chaumont in early March 1814 the British, who had so far kept out of the actual fighting, persuaded their allies that their anti-Napoleonic alliance should last for 20 years.

There was at last a new spirit of co-operation between Britain and the three continental powers, Russia, Austria and Prussia. Unlike Metternich, Robert Stewart, Viscount Castlereagh (1769–1822), the British Foreign Secretary, was not concerned about the spread of noxious revolutionary doctrines from Napoleonic France: what worried him was the prospect that Napoleonic France's domination of the continent might continue. Although the young English Romantics came to see him as the architect of oppression, Castlereagh saw himself as the architect of peace. But first there must be more fighting, in which Britain would from now on play its part not just as lender, a role that it had played under Pitt, but also as participant. There had been coalitions in the past that Napoleon had always managed to break up. This time the coalition, if all members kept to the agreement fashioned at Chaumont, could not be prised apart. On 4 March the treaty was signed. Just over a week later the British showed that they too could be effective on land, fighting alongside the Spanish to drive the French from Spain. On 12 May the British raised the fleur-de-lis of the ancestral kings of France in the port of Bordeaux. The British, like their allies, were already in France.

The end came quickly. On 30 March, after a last fight at Montmartre, the hill overlooking the capital, Marshal Marmont signed the capitulation of Paris. The next day Napoleon, *en route* for the

Napoleon signs his abdication at the palace of Fontainebleau

capital, reached the palace of Fontainebleau, a day's ride away. Joseph had already arranged for the court, including the Empress, to leave for Rambouillet to the west of Paris. Talleyrand stayed behind, having forgotten, so he said at the city barrier, to bring his passport with him. Marie-Louise wrote to reassure her husband that she had wanted to stay in the capital, but was running away because she had been led to believe that their son, the King of Rome, might be in danger. As Russian troops entered Paris, few Parisians showed any enthusiasm for a restoration of the Bourbons and the white bands that signified allegiance to the royalist white flag were on the wrists of invading soldiers.

Napoleon was convinced that the army would stand by him, until generals, including Ney, told him that he was wrong. Two marshals, Marmont and Etienne-Jacques-Joseph-Alexandre MacDonald (1765–1840) were asked to go to Paris with a notice of his provisional abdication in favour of his son. Once there Marmont, one of his oldest friends, abandoned him. On 6 April, persuaded again by the marshals, Napoleon abdicated unconditionally. That day Talleyrand persuaded the Senate, for years the passive instrument of Napoleon's will, to petition for the return of Louis XVI's oldest surviving brother, who had long borne the title of Louis XVIII. On 11 April 1814 Napoleon signed the treaty of Fontainebleau, which left him with his title, a projected income of 2 million francs from the French government and his own little domain, Elba. The man who had aspired to run a continent would be back where he started, on an island.

Following his abdication, the allies concluded the Treaty of Paris, by which France gave up her claims to the southern and northern Netherlands, Germany, Switzerland, Italy and Malta, surrendered some colonies to Britain, which had spent the later years of the conflict filching overseas territories controlled by France and its allies, kept its 1789 borders while acquiring part of the Rhineland and part of Savoy. It had to pay no reparations, put up with no foreign troops and was allowed to hold onto the artistic treasures it had stolen. As Napoleon had rejected an earlier and more favourable treaty proposed to him the previous year by Metternich, this was generous.

The fallen emperor hoped his wife and son would join him at Fontainebleau but they did not; he was sure that if they joined his father-in-law, the Emperor Francis, he would never see them again. He chatted to his Foreign Minister, Louis, marquis de Caulaincourt (1773–1827), went upstairs to bed and then sent down to summon Caulaincourt to tell him he had tried to poison himself. The poison was too old and did not work and, after vomiting, Napoleon recovered. On 20 April he slowly descended the grand Renaissance horseshoe staircase to the main courtyard of the white horse, the Cour du Cheval Blanc, where he saw the Old Guard lined up. While soldiers sobbed, he embraced their general and then kissed their flag, saying *May this kiss pass on into all your hearts*.[38] Having promised to write a book about their story, he flung himself into the waiting carriage and was off. At Fréjus he sent word ahead to Elba's commandant with a message for the inhabitants: *Tell them that I have chosen their island for my residence because I know the kindness of their character and the excellence of their climate. They will always be an object of the liveliest interest to me.*[39] His account of events was a little fanciful, as his enemies had chosen his home for him, but he did not mind. He was still good at making people love him and he would make his exile work.

Napoleon's fall was even more rapid than his rise. Only 18 months separate his arrival in Moscow from the last scenes at Fontainebleau. Some point out that he had taught his enemies too well how to combat him, others that he was

Auguste Viesse de Marmont (1774–1852), one of Napoleon's oldest friends, was made Duke of Ragusa (the Italian name for Dubrovnik) by Napoleon but from 1814 to 1830 served the Bourbons. Parisian wags invented a verb meaning to betray: *raguser*. Je raguse, tu raguses, il raguse … (I betray, you betray, he betrays …).

temperamentally incapable of waging a defensive war, yet others that his method of fighting demanded that he fight on hostile land. He had lost so many horses on the Russian campaign he could never replace them and, though France could raise more men than any other European country, in 1813 and 1814 he had to work with raw recruits, too old or too young to be adequate fighters. In the conservative west of the country there were signs that the peasants had had enough of his endless demands for conscripts.

There were also signs of the kind of deterioration that occurs in men who have been in power, especially absolute power, too long. He would not listen to any objections to his ideas, he was impatient with flatterers but he also did not want to be contradicted and his habit of optimism had made him unrealistic. His hold over his subordinates was still remarkable, however. The evidence of her letters shows that his young wife, Marie-Louise, was in love with him when he was with her, and, if his rages were terrifying, his smiles exercised an irresistible attraction.

What is certain is that there were signs of physical decay. As a young man, Napoleon had been a pale, thin, sallow workaholic: small, mercurial and exhausting. After Tilsit he became less physically active; after Wagram, when he had three years without a campaign, he became softer, slower and fatter. In the Russian campaign, he stayed on and on in Moscow simply hoping, in vain, for something to turn up. Along with his new paunch came a new hesitancy.

He never lost his remarkable capacity for remembering detail. In September 1805, for example, during the march from the Rhine to the Danube, he met a unit that had got detached from its parent formation and, even though the Grand Army numbered 200,000, he was able to tell the commander, who had mislaid his orders, exactly where he should be on the next three nights. But there were moments when he could not see his way through the detail. He became listless and depressed, succumbing to bouts of inertia after the battles of Aspern and Wagram in 1809 and agreeing to the summer armistice of 1813, when his enemies were in a worse state than he was. In 1812–14 he fought as he had fought in 1796–7. He had learned nothing new. Even he could not cope with truly enormous armies, neither when he had one, as in summer 1812, nor when he fought against one, as in autumn 1813.

Few rulers have had so many bright ideas as he had about how to run a country or a continent, but he was too preoccupied with too many concerns to see his projects through. His immense prestige meant that for many years the French political class stuck to his concepts, working with the concordat he had signed with the Pope, developing his great museum of the Louvre, applying his theories to a national system of education, cultivating an elite to manage things in the arts, the sciences and government, rewarding merit and dispensing justice as he saw fit. He had made France a Napoleonic country. In 1814 he had to leave France to its own devices and had put himself at the mercy of a Bourbon, Louis XVIII, a tired, slow-moving, shrewd and cautious man. Waiting to see what would happen would be a test of his own patience; and patience was a quality scarcely evident in his previous behaviour.

The making of a legend 1815–21

Elba was never an island paradise. The inhabitants scraped a living from mining or fishing. For a man of Napoleon's energy, intelligence and ambition, Elba was too small, too remote and too provincial. He was devastated to hear that Joséphine had died on 29 May 1814, having caught a chill after a visit from the Tsar to Malmaison. For two days he stayed alone in his room. His mistress Maria Walewska came to see him with Alexandre their son, whom he was delighted to play with, but he soon sent her away. Maybe he hoped to give Marie-Louise no excuse for not sharing his exile. If so, the stratagem failed, for she was easily seduced by the charming one-eyed womaniser, Count Adam Adalbert von Neipperg (1775–1829), whom Metternich, himself an arch-womaniser, had deliberately provided as her aide-de-camp. In 1815 Marie-Louise wrote one last letter to Napoleon. He had to accept that he would never see her or his son. Two of his sisters, Elise and Caroline, had also deserted him. Of the Bonaparte women he was supported by just two, his mother and his sister Pauline; and it was Pauline, the most foolish, most promiscuous of the girls, who was also the most loyal. To give her brother funds to help him return to France, she would sell her elegant Hôtel Charost in Paris to the Duke of Wellington. In this way one of the finest of Bonaparte homes became one the most beautiful of British embassies.

On Elba Napoleon was short of money. The new King had no intention of giving Napoleon the 2 million francs a year he was supposed to receive from the French government. Napoleon had his own fortune, but had no way of adding to it. He expected to live in an imperial style, with a handful of courtiers and a small band of guards, both civilians and soldiers in distinctive smart uniforms. After a while, however, the pleasures of reorganising the administration, arranging for rubbish collections in his new capital, Portoferraio, paving the streets, lighting them at night, adding a storey to his house and revamping the gardens began to pall. He could see that soon there would no need of any more plans. He became bored.

All was not well in France. The old nobles who flocked to the Tuileries Palace to announce their loyalty to the King despised the parvenu Napoleonic nobles with grandiloquent titles and were careful to make them feel inferior. Napoleon's soldiers were also no longer wanted. They were put on half-pay and frequently royalist gentlemen who had little experience or who had fought for France's enemies replaced officers who had followed the imperial eagle into Italy, Spain, Germany, Poland and Russia.

Napoleonic symbols were everywhere, on columns in city squares and on triumphal arches; the nation's children had learnt by heart the imperial catechism that inculcated obedience to the Emperor; art galleries were full of the treasures looted by the Emperor from other nations. The people resented the presence of hostile armies in France; and, whatever Talleyrand liked to suggest, but for the foreigners the Bourbons could not have been restored. The new government was an alien institution, run largely by people who did not know modern France and had no desire to know it.

Napoleon was in constant touch with what was happening through his spies and other correspondents. The idea of returning to France attracted both his gambler's instinct and his sense of mission. His mother and his sister encouraged him; his frustrations convinced him he had no alternative. The only point to decide was when to go and how to get to Paris. The opportune moment came in late February 1815, when Sir Neil Campbell (1776–1827), the British commandant on the island, appointed to watch over Napoleon, went to Florence for a medical appointment. Napoleon quickly took a boat to the mainland and landed at Golfe Juan near Antibes. He headed northeast for the mountains. In winter the roads were icy and his reception in any of the large towns might be cool. Napoleon and his men, numbering several hundred assorted Frenchmen, Corsicans and Poles, endured the harsh conditions cheerfully. Confronted by French troops in the service of the King at a small village near Grenoble, he had his band play the Marseillaise and, then walking towards the infantry with their guns at the ready, opened his coat and cried out, *Here I am. Kill your Emperor if you wish.* They all cheered, 'Vive l'Empereur' (Long live the Emperor).[40]

After that incident his journey towards Paris turned into a procession. At Grenoble itself the garrison opened the city gates to him and he soon found he was heading an army of 8,000 men. In Lyon, which the King's brother Artois had just deserted, the silk workers welcomed him. At Auxerre, Ney, who had boasted that he would bring Napoleon back to Paris in an iron cage, joined his former master. Napoleon declared that he would be in Paris for 20 March to celebrate his son's birthday and on that day, to the applause of a large crowd, he duly mounted the steps of the Tuileries. He was convinced that Frenchmen were thrilled to have him back. The King had raced away as fast as his huge body would allow him. All Napoleon needed to do was to convince dissident fellow countrymen that he stood for freedom and the rest of Europe that he stood for peace.

At Vienna the major powers, who were meeting in a congress to bring lasting peace to Europe, had almost come to blows. Russia and its chief client Prussia were quarrelling with Britain, its main ally Austria and its new friend Bourbon France over the redrawing of the map of the continent, when the diplomats, hearing that their common enemy was back, stopped bickering at once. The big four, together with Spain, Portugal and Sweden, committed themselves to the defeat of Napoleon, whose march on Paris proved that his authority was illegitimate, based as it must be solely on popularity within France. Whereas the Romanovs, Hohenzollerns, Habsburgs, Hanoverians, Bourbons (of two kinds), Braganças and Vasas (the last of the kind before the Bernadottes) stood for the universally accepted principle of hereditary right, Napoleon claimed his authority rested on the general will of a nation.

Benjamin Constant (1767–1830) persuaded Napoleon that he must stand for the forgotten republican concept of liberty. He duly passed the Acte Additionnel, which modified the imperial constitution, as a reaction to the liberal Charter that Louis XVIII had granted on assuming the throne in 1814. Now Napoleon too conceded freedom of the press, civil liberty and a bicameral legislature (parliamentary government in France was a Bourbon creation). The franchise, in the standard liberal way, was restricted to the better off. In this way Napoleon annoyed many of his most ardent followers, the dispossessed, without reassuring the middle classes, who were worried by a demonstration of workers and former soldiers in favour of the principles of 1793. Though Napoleon had sought to have his decisions supported by referenda – which he had skilfully manipulated – the motor of government from 1804 to 1814, if not before, had essentially been his will. Now, however, he had implied that he ruled by consent. He was both a revolutionary and a liberal.

The contradictory nature of Napoleon's appeal ultimately reinforced the legend that he unified France, but immediately it caused him problems. When he put the new constitution to a referendum, the 'yes' vote fell to just over 1.5 million, less than half the figure he had achieved when asking for an endorsement of the Empire in 1804. When there was an election for the assembly envisaged by the new constitution, the majority of its members were opposed to war. In order to survive, however, Napoleon knew he must attack the allied armies quickly before they had deployed the large forces they could muster. In 1813 he had not been able to use valuable men in Germany because he had used them to garrison key German towns. Now in 1815 he was not sure of the conservative west, so he left a large force behind in the Vendée, where in the 1790s hundreds of thousands of Vendéans had died resisting republican recruiting and religious revolution.

Napoleon's last campaign was one of his most dramatic. To defeat all his enemies, he first had to cope with the British and the Prussians in the southern Netherlands before tackling the Austrians and the Russians, who would be much slower to approach France. His reappearance had clarified people's thoughts. Some members of the family had abandoned him in 1814. The resentful Lucien, the serpentine Caroline and her flamboyant, foolish Murat now rallied to him. Of other marshals Ney, Davout and Soult stood by him, whereas Bernadotte, now Crown Prince of Sweden, Massena and Marmont were committed opponents. Two of his most devious ministers, Talleyrand the refined diplomat and Fouché the harsh head of the police, were too involved with the Bourbons to retract and, when they appeared on either side of the King, they were described as Vice and Crime. It was only among ordinary soldiers that Napoleon could count on unquestioning loyalty to himself; and now he would test their fidelity to the limit.

Napoleon promised that if France were left unmolested, he would stay within the boundaries set by the Treaty of Paris after his abdication. But no important statesman outside France believed his promises any more. Meanwhile Murat, who had declared war on France in 1814 and been allowed by the Austrians to keep Naples as a reward for his defection, now in March 1815 switched sides again and declared war on Austria. If the first move had been opportunistic, the second was idiotic. Eventually he was captured in southern Italy by the Bourbon Neapolitan army and on 13

October he was shot. By then Napoleon's own adventure was long over. Murat's foolishness was merely a distraction.

The main action took place much closer to one of France's borders. Napoleon had two alternative strategies: either to wait for the allies to strike while he built up his own forces or to strike before the allies had time to deploy their forces. If he were to wait to be attacked, then he would fight in France, which had been unpopular in 1814. Besides, Napoleon was a master of the art of attack. He did not realise that in taking on Wellington, he was up against a man expert in the science of defence.

Napoleon's plan was to split the British and the Prussians, chase off the Prussians, then turn on the British. He was at the north-eastern frontier of France on 14 June before his presence was suspected and on 15 June the French crossed the River Sambre. The next day Napoleon defeated the Prussians at Ligny and subsequently ordered a new marshal, Emmanuel marquis de Grouchy (1766–1847), to drive them away to the east. Meanwhile Ney was supposed to hold the British at Quatre-Bras till Napoleon, victorious over the Prussians, would arrive to rout them. Instead, with the help of a thunderstorm, Wellington was able to withdraw in good order before Napoleon arrived.

Wellington chose to stop on Mont-Saint-Jean, a defensive position that well suited the style of fighting he had perfected in the Iberian peninsula, in particular the use of reverse slopes to hide his troops behind hillocks, so that just as enemy soldiers crested the top of a rise, they would find themselves confronted by lines of infantry ready to decimate them with volley after volley of shot. Only Napoleon's famed artillery was likely to dislodge the mixed army of Britons, Dutchmen and Hanoverians, but heavy rain had rendered the ground soft, making Napoleon's shot less likely to ricochet and therefore much less lethal.

Just as he began to order the batteries to fire, he was told that a Prussian force was in sight. At this stage Napoleon could have withdrawn, but he did not. He had detached a large force under Grouchy to cope with the main Prussian army; now, though it was clear that the Prussians had evaded him and had arrived on the main battlefield, Grouchy followed his orders rather than returning to help Napoleon. Had Grouchy shown the kind of initiative that Desaix showed at Marengo, the result of Waterloo might have been different, but Grouchy was no Desaix. At the crisis of the battle he was nowhere near the action.

Napoleon almost prised apart the British defence, almost broke the line, almost triumphed before the Prussians arrived. As evening fell, the British were still resisting, so he ordered the Imperial Guard to lead a final assault. One last time the reverse slope technique was used with devastating effect. The Guard was broken and their retreat soon became a rout, at least for as long as the exhausted British could chase after them. Wellington's army had saved the allies from defeat. Blücher's army now set about achieving a victory. Memories of their own catastrophic rout at Jena in 1806 had taught the Prussians how to pursue a defeated enemy. By the time Wellington and Blücher met, around nine o'clock, eight hours after Napoleon's troops had opened fire, the Imperial army had disintegrated.

Napoleon, exhausted, hurried back to Paris. He still wrote to his brother Joseph about using another army, but he rejected the advice of his brother Lucien to dissolve the liberal Legislature and proclaim himself dictator. He refused. On 21 June he abdicated in favour of his son.

The members of his Legislature would not have it and his Austrian father-in-law, who had taken charge of Napoleon 'II', would never have allowed it. On 3 July his Minister of War, Davout, signed the capitulation of the capital. On 8 July Louis XVIII returned to Paris, a ruler of France imposed on the country for the second time by France's foes. The new Treaty of Paris drawn up in November was much tougher than the first. France had to

The last battle. Napoleon's retreat from Waterloo, after a painting by Steuben

surrender its Rhineland fortresses to Prussia, its part of Savoy to Piedmont. The country had to pay an indemnity of 700 million francs within five years, have its eastern departments occupied by foreign troops for from three to five years and return Napoleon's looted art. While David, Napoleon's chief painter, felt too committed to the Emperor to stay in France and went into voluntary exile in Brussels, the director of the Louvre, Vivant Denon, stayed on until 3 October to try to keep as many works of art as he could in France, but he could not prevent the Venetians from getting back the horses of St Mark's nor the Pope from recovering his antique statues.

For Napoleon himself there would be a final twist to the story. For a while he lingered unmolested near Paris and stayed with his step-daughter Hortense in Joséphine's house at Malmaison. He had time to see two bastard sons, one of them Alexandre Walewski, and three former mistresses, one of them Maria Walewska. He said goodbye to his mother. He made arrangements for his money with the banker Jacques Laffitte (1767–1844). He had a more pressing problem: where would he live? His brother Joseph escaped to America, his stepson Eugène sought refuge with his wife's family in Bavaria, the Pope, now restored to the eternal city, offered many members of the family a base in Rome. Had he been left to the Prussians, Napoleon might have been killed. He made up his mind to appeal to the British. He drafted a letter to the Prince Regent, the future George IV: *Your Royal Highness: victimised by the factions which divide my country, and by the hostility of the greatest European powers, I have ended my political career; and I come, as Themistocles did, to seat myself by the hearth of the British people. I put myself under the protection of its laws – a protection which I claim from Your Royal Highness, as the strongest, the stubbornest, and the most generous of my foes.*[43]

Napoleon admired Jacques-Louis David (1748–1825), who called Napoleon 'my hero'.[41] Of the portrait of himself in his study at 4.13 am, he said *at night I am concerned with the happiness of my subjects and in the day I work for their glory.*[42] Working at night helped undermine his health.

Napoleon's reference to a notable Athenian politician seeking asylum from an alien king may have flattered the recipient of the letter, but Napoleon never received a reply. After five days of reflection he decided to surrender to the captain of the British warship HMS *Bellerophon*, which had fought at Aboukir Bay and Trafalgar. He was treated well and even saw the southern coast of England, but he was never permitted to land, for his Whig friends had thought of using a writ of Habeas Corpus to have him released and the Tory government was keen to evade such legal niceties. The other powers later agreed that the British could put him where they thought fit. Already they had decided to exile him to St Helena, an island in the South Atlantic, as far away from the shores of Europe as possible. If he died there, France and all Europe would be free of him forever.

The ships bearing Napoleon and his entourage into exile arrive at St Helena and the harbour of Jamestown

Napoleon's adventures in 1815 have been referred to as the Hundred Days. The figures do not add up. He left Elba on 26 February, disembarked on the French coast on 1 March, was defeated at Waterloo on 18 June, abdicated in Paris on 22 June and left France forever on 15 July. The idea of the Hundred Days, however, has become so fixed in popular memory that it has been applied to the first weeks of the first presidency of Franklin Roosevelt and thereafter to the start of many new regimes. What remains true is that the period was short, dramatic and decisive, and soon the central element in the development of the Napoleonic legend.

The story of Napoleon's life on St Helena, where he arrived on 15 October, is well documented and perhaps has become better known than any other stage in his life. He began his exile at the Briars, home of the agent of the East India Company, William Balcombe, and enjoyed a charming flirtation with the younger of Balcombe's two daughters, Betsy (died 1873). Once it was ready for him, he moved to Longwood, the summer seat of the lieutenant-governor of the island. He made an effort to learn English, but languages were not his forte and he soon gave up. For a time he was an enthusiastic gardener.

His paramount concern, however, was shaping the accounts of his life that the people who saw him daily would bequeath to future generations. It was reasonable to expect that his companions in exile should think of writing their memoirs. In addition to Barry O'Meara (1780–1836), who acted as his doctor and spied on him for the British, his hero-worshipping valet Louis Marchand and his servant Ali, there were those whom Jean Tulard, doyen of modern Napoleonic historians, has christened 'the four evangelists': Las Cases, Gourgaud, Montholon and Bertrand. For them Napoleon acted and spoke so that through his last chroniclers future generations would know his story and, knowing it, would believe in him.

The chief storytellers or mythmakers make up a disparate group whose stories have become known slowly over a period of over 100 years. The first version of the *Mémorial de Ste Hélène* of Emmanuel de Las Cases (1766–1842), a confidant of Napoleon on St Helena, though a royalist by inclination, was published in 1823 and went through many subsequent editions. By contrast the memoirs of Charles Tristan Comte de Montholon (1782–1853), the head of the household at Longwood, did not appear until 1847, those of Gaspard Gourgaud (1783–1852) not until 1899 and those of Henri-Gratien Bertrand (1773–1844) not until after the Second World War.

For this reason alone the memoirs of Las Cases have been more influential in creating the received picture of Napoleon, but he was also able to weave Napoleon's chaotic ramblings into a coherent pattern of observations and reminiscences. The Napoleon who emerges from his account was not the ogre discerned by his enemies but a sage recollecting his triumphs in tranquillity, plausibly glossing over his failures, prophetically sketching the world he would like to see created. He dreamed of united Italy and united Germany, of a Poland free from Russia, of an Ireland independent of Britain. If he had seemed a little dictatorial in France, that was because of the immaturity of the people. His intentions had always been liberal. He stood for human rights, for religious tolerance – he was only too willing to explain the essential differences between Christianity and Islam – and for a sound legal system – he wished to keep the Code as simple as possible, but the lawyers saw endless difficulties.

What became clear on St Helena is that the Napoleon who during the Hundred Days had become a defender of citizens' rights and freedoms would endure. When his nephew and eventual heir, Louis-Napoleon, published his *Idées Napoléoniennes* in 1839, most of the book was concerned with a Napoleonic political vision for France and for Europe, not with warfare; and when he came to power, first as Prince-President in 1848, then after a coup as the Emperor Napoleon III in 1852, he would proclaim to France's sceptical neighbours that the Empire stood for peace. Las Cases had done his work well; and yet, paradoxically, Napoleon continued to fascinate Frenchmen because, unlike the drab and boring Bourbons who replaced him, he had given them glory.

Napoleon's daily life at Longwood gave little scope for a man who had ruled France from the cavernous rooms of the Tuileries Palace and who directed the fate of nations from his battle tent. He now presided over a tiny and quarrelsome court. His chief cause of complaint, however, soon came to be not any one of his entourage, but the English governor, Sir Hudson Lowe (1769–1844).

Lowe arrived in April 1816. An insecure man, whose chief claim to fame was that he had organised a band of Corsican royalist soldiers who loathed the French, he worried about rules. Napoleon was not to be called Emperor, so when an admirer inscribed a book to him with the words 'Imperatori Napoleoni', which in classical Latin meant 'to General Napoleon', Lowe would not give it to Napoleon because he was told that in later Latin 'Imperatori' could mean 'to the Emperor'. He insisted that Napoleon reduce his staff from 15 to 11, that he cut his annual expenditure to £8,000 and that all correspondence should go through him.

In exile on St Helena, Napoleon dictates his memoirs to Emmanuel
Dieudonne, Comte de Las Cases

Napoleon began to enjoy his propaganda war against Lowe. To show how mean Lowe was, he ostentatiously had his best silver sold to a jeweller in Jamestown, the capital. When Lowe rebuked Napoleon for spending too much money on coal – Napoleon hated the cold and loved soaking in hot baths – Napoleon burnt some of the furniture as fuel. The attempt to cut Napoleon off from his correspondents failed. Message after message got through to the Francophile and Whig Fox household at Holland House in London, which, as in the days of Charles James Fox (1749–1806), was the main conduit through which Napoleon's cause was publicised in Britain. Henry Fox, third Baron Holland (1773–1840) and nephew of Charles James, raised embarrassing points in the House of Lords and, though he lost the vote, the government raised Bonaparte's allowance to £12,000.

For a time Napoleon had reason to be pleased. He was the victim, he was sure. As early as 1816 Las Cases had written to Lucien Bonaparte to protest against his brother's treatment, for which offence Las Cases had been sent back to Europe and his papers confiscated until after Napoleon's death. The final memory of Napoleon, as he himself had wanted, would be of a lingering martyr to British insensitivity. It was a better fate than the one Field Marshal Blücher had wished for him: immediate execution.

Napoleon stayed at Longwood until he died on 5 May 1821. Talleyrand commented that his death was just news, not an event; outside fervently Bonapartist circles, Napoleon already belonged to a receding past. But he was soon again an inspiration to world-weary Romantics like Lord Byron (1788–1824) and Stendhal, or to old soldiers who treasured their guns, their swords and their decorations, or to anyone who believed that he had worked to make France both glorious and free.

To such people in his last years he appears as the victim of the callousness of the British and the pettiness of the Bourbons. Why had he died so young, when he was only 51? The official verdict was that like his father he had died of cancer of the stomach, but doubts were caused by traces of arsenic in his hair. One theory is that in the damp climate of Saint Helena the arsenic that was normally in wallpaper seeped into his body when he was not feeling well and so was confined too much to the house. The other theory is more sensational: he was poisoned on purpose. The poisoner could have been British, but the prime candidate has become Montholon, who had gradually seen all rivals for the Emperor's attention removed, or Marchand, who gave him food and drink. The case against either of them, however, cannot be proved.

Napoleon was buried at his request in a remote grave in Geranium Valley on the island. In his will, however, he wrote, *I desire that my ashes repose on the banks of the Seine in the midst of the French people whom I have loved so much*;[44] and this request was carried out in 1840, when Britain had a Whig government that would not object and France had as its head of state a king 'of the French' who set himself the task of reconciling royalist and revolutionary France.

During the Second World War the Dutch historian Pieter Geyl, aware of the then fashionable analogy between Napoleon and Hitler, laid out with great skill the debate among French historians, who had already been squabbling over Napoleon's reputation for over a hundred years, like jackals over dead prey. As a general Napoleon is still admired for the conduct of his first Italian campaign in 1796 and for the victory at Austerlitz in 1805, for which he may rank with von Moltke, who routed the French in the Franco-Prussian war of 1870, and with Heinz Guderian (1888–1954) whose *blitzkrieg* routed the British and French in 1940. But he was less successful trying to engineer a decisive battle on the plains of Russia in 1812 or when faced with superior numbers in 1813 or struggling to break down Wellington's defensive tactics in 1815. Over the course of his military career, while his opponents learned how to counter him, he failed to learn new methods. After

1809 he also deteriorated physically, so that he was seldom as dynamic as he once had been.

As a ruler he was promising rather than accomplished. He was good at seeing a problem and imposing a solution. He never had the time to make his changes permanent and, if he left so strong a mark on France and on much of the continent, for example in the laws of inheritance, that is because of the work of future generations. He has been blamed for ending the period when France had dominated the continent, a period that went back at least to the personal rule of Louis XIV; after him France was too exhausted to cope with the rise of Prussia. It is true too that after 1815 France's population and its economy grew much more slowly than the populations and economies of Britain and Germany; and this has often been blamed on the way that Napoleon's Code decided how property should be divided between heirs. But in 1950–75, while the same laws were still in force, France's population and economy grew rapidly. Population growth depends more on morale than on law.

Napoleon wanted France to be governed by military and civilian elites; many of the successes and failures of France since 1815 may be traced back to the dominance of those groups. He also had the popular touch, so that when he looked for the support of his countrymen or his soldiers, he knew how to make an appeal to the majority, whether through a plebiscite or by making an exciting gesture. He was a master of propaganda, who first created newspapers to bolster his cause in Italy and Egypt and then was careful to present his edited version of events in the periodic bulletins of the Army and the government publication, the *Moniteur*.

He appealed to people's vanity and sense of worth by awarding the Legion of Honour and by creating ever more grandiose titles for his officials; and yet he also encouraged useful learning, so that France retained its prestige in all matters scientific. He had no time for the excessive influence of hereditary nobilities in Britain;

and he knew the situation was much worse in Russia, Prussia, Austria and Spain. He wanted those who served the state to be chosen for their ability as administrators and he started to plan a kind of education that was open to the talents that France needed. He saw the need for a stable economy, but was less good at encouraging enterprise.

Ultimately the attraction of Napoleon derived from his personal magnetism. Those who met him never forgot him. Though he was frequently callous to women, including Joséphine, they were usually ready to forgive him. The men whom he led through terrible privations venerated him. Even his enemies like Talleyrand, Metternich and Wellington conceded that he was remarkable; the kindly Pius VII, whom he had treated abominably, was ready to intervene to help him and his family. For almost a generation he was the most important person in France and in Europe. Even if it is true, as Tolstoy claims in *War and Peace*, that he was often mastered by events, not their master, the world he strove to master had been changed forever.

Notes

The principal sources of the story of Napoleon are his own writings. Jean Tulard, the doyen of Napoleonic studies today, has recalled that from his youth Napoleon wrote a lot and the habit never left him. He aspired to be a novelist and the more cynical may think that his early leaning towards fiction affected much of his later writing. He wrote much of his own propaganda – he was responsible for many newspaper articles from the time of the first Italian campaign in 1796 down to the final campaign of 1815 – and, when he was not writing, he was dictating, a habit that proved useful when he devoted himself to the task of creating his own image for future generations while a prisoner on St Helena. As for his letters, Tulard has estimated that Napoleon himself wrote about 20,000 in all, most of which have survived.

Long before his last exile, Napoleon had also generated a host of memorialists, from his early secretary Bourrienne to the competing members of his entourage who were with him in the last years of his life. Napoleon's character is often best captured in their anecdotes; and these have been passed on from one writer to the next. It is not always easy to track down the source of a quotation, so sometimes I have referred to a source where I read of the incident or remark. A good selection of Napoleon's letters in English was collected, edited and translated by J M Thompson more than 50 years ago and it is still in print today. Most of the letters are available in the 32-volume edition sponsored by his nephew, Napoleon III. There are selections, as of his love letters to Joséphine; and Lucian Regenbogen has produced a book of his sayings.

1   Vincent Cronin, *Napoleon* (Fontana, London: 1990) p 33.
2   Cronin, *Napoleon*, p 34.
3   J M Thompson (ed), *Napoleon's Letters* (J M Dent & Sons, London: 1954) pp 32–3.
4   Emmanuel de Las Cases, *Mémorial de Sainte-Hélène* (1823) vol II, p 1282, hereafter Las Cases.
5   Las Cases, vol II, p 1016.
6   Thompson (ed), *Napoleon's Letters*, p 40.
7   Lucian Regenbogen, *Napoléon a dit* (Les Belles Lettres, Paris: 1996) p 337, hereafter Regenbogen.
8   Regenbogen, p 80.
9   Regenbogen, p 29.
10 Regenbogen, p 349.
11 *Correspondance de Napoléon I* (32 vols, Paris: 1858–70) vol I, p 72, hereafter *Correspondance*.
12 Napoléon, *Lettres d'amour à Joséphine*, ed Chantal de Tourtier-Bonazzi (Fayard, Paris: 1981) p 46, hereafter *Lettres d'amour à Joséphine*.
13 *Lettres d'amour à Joséphine*, pp 51, 52, 55, 64, 74, 103, 125.
14 Las Cases, vol II, p 1016.
15 Regenbogen, p 57.
16 Regenbogen, p 85.
17 Las Cases, vol I, p 495.
18 J Christopher Herold, *Bonaparte in Egypt* (Hamish Hamilton, London: 1963) p 319.
19 *Correspondance*, vol XXIX, p 450.
20 Las Cases, vol II, p 1162.
21 Regenbogen, p 245.
22 *Correspondance*, vol VI, No 5090.

23 Regenbogen, p 142.

24 *Correspondance*, vol XI, No 9538.

25 Letter written in January 1806, quoted by E Hales, *Napoleon and the Pope* (Eyre & Spottiswoode, London: 1962) p 94.

26 *Lettres d'amour à Joséphine*, p 242.

27 Thompson (ed), *Napoleon's Letters*, p 159.

28 Regenbogen, p 146.

29 Regenbogen, p 141.

30 Louis Bergeron, *France under Napoleon* (Princeton University Press, Princeton: 1981) p 34.

31 Regenbogen, p 188.

32 Regenbogen, p 392.

33 Simon Schama, *Patriots and Liberators* (Alfred A Knopf, New York: 1977) p 490.

34 G Lefebvre, *Napoléon* (Paris: 1963) p 438.

35 Regenbogen, p 345.

36 Thompson (ed), *Napoleon's Letters*, p 274.

37 *Correspondance*, vol XXV, No 20018.

38 Cited, among others, by Regenbogen, p 209.

39 Regenbogen, p 209.

40 Cited, among many, by Dominique de Villepin, *Les Cent-Jours* (Perrin, Paris: 2001) p 212.

41 E J Delécluze, *David, son école, son temps* (Paris: 1855) p 204.

42 Delécluze, *David, son école, son temps*, p 347.

43 *Correspondance*, vol XXVIII, No 22066.

44 Regenbogen, p 269.

Year	Age	Life
1769		15 August: Birth of Napoleon Buonaparte in Ajaccio, Corsica.
1779	9	1 January: Arrives at school in Autun. 15 May: Transfers to cadet school at Brienne.
1784	15	22 October: Enters Ecole Militaire in Paris.
1785	16	24 February: Carlo Buonaparte (father) dies of cancer of the stomach. 28 October: Leaves Ecole Militaire as artillery lieutenant.
1786	17	15 August: Arrives in Ajaccio. On leave in Corsica for 21 months.
1788	19	1 January: Returns to Ajaccio. 1 June: Leaves Corsica for Auxonne.
1789	20	9 September: Leaves for Corsica.

Year	History	Culture
1769	First partition of Poland. Arthur Wellesley, later Duke of Wellington, born.	Fragonard, 'The Study'. Joshua Reynolds knighted.
1779	Captain Cook murdered in Hawaii. Spanish declare war on Britain, siege of Gibraltar begins.	Samuel Johnson, *Lives of the Poets*. Hume, *Dialogues of Natural Religion*.
1784	Treaty of Constantinople: Ottoman Empire agrees to Russian annexation of the Crimea. British treaty with Tipu Sahib, Sultan of Mysore.	Goya, 'Don Manuel de Zuniga'. Death of Samuel Johnson.
1785	Warren Hastings resigns as Governor-General of India. Marie Antoinette discredited in Diamond Necklace affair.	David, 'Oath of the Horatii'.
1786	Lord Cornwallis made Governor-General of India. Death of Frederick the Great of Prussia.	Mozart, *The Marriage of Figaro*. Burns, *Poems chiefly in the Scottish dialect*.
1788	Louis XVI calls Estates-General. United States Constitution comes into force.	David, 'Love of Paris and Helena'. *The Times* first published in London.
1789	Meeting of Estates General (later National Assembly). 14 July: Fall of the Bastille. Declaration of the Rights of Man. 6 October: Women march to Versailles; Louis XVI moved to Tuileries palace. George Washington inaugurated as President of the USA.	Blake, *Songs of Innocence*.

Year	Age	Life
1790	21	In Corsica – attempt to return to France foiled by bad weather. Joseph elected to municipal council.
1791	22	In Valence and, 11 February, in Auxonne, then 16 June back to Valence. October: death of uncle Archdeacon Lucien. Napoleon and Joseph buy a house in Ajaccio.
1792	23	31 March: Elected lieutenant-colonel, Corsican volunteers. 10 August: In Paris during assault on Tuileries palace. 15 October: Back in Ajaccio.
1793	24	Quarrels with Paoli. Arrives in Toulon, which is soon handed over to the British. 17–18 December: Leads successful night assault to retake l'Eguilette overlooking Toulon harbour. Made brigadier-general.

Year	History	Culture
1790	Paoli returns to Corsica. Re-organisation of France into departments. Civic constitution of the clergy.	Burke, *Reflections on the Revolution in France.* Mozart, *Cosi fan tutte.*
1791	Louis XVI's flight to Varennes. Massacre of Champs de Mars. Legislative Assembly meets.	Paine, *The Rights of Man* (to 1792). Boswell, *Life of Johnson.*
1792	First use of guillotine. France declares war on Austria. Prussia declares war on France. August: Attack on Tuileries – fall of monarchy. September massacres in Paris prisons. Proclamation of the French Republic. French victories of Valmy and Jemappes	Mary Wollstonecraft, *A Vindication of the Rights of Women.*
1793	Execution of Louis XVI. France declares war on Britain and the Netherlands (war of First Coalition). Revolt in the Vendée. Fall of the Girondins – the beginnings of the federalist revolts all over France. Danton leaves the Committee of Public Safety. Robespierre joins it. Drawn battle of Hondschoote. French victory at Wattignies. Execution of Marie-Antoinette and of the Girondins. Second Partition of Poland.	David, *The Murder of Marat.*

Year	Age	Life
1794	25	Imprisoned in Antibes following the fall of Robespierre. Renounces Jacobinism. 20 August: Released from prison.
1795	26	5 October: Suppresses rebellion in Paris with 'whiff of grape-shot'. Made general in command of the Army of the Interior.
1796	27	9 March: Marries Joséphine (Rose) de Beauharnais. Made general of the Army of Italy. 11 March: Leaves for Italy. 10 May: Wins battle of Lodi. During campaign that follows, is based on Milan. 15–17 November: Wins battle of Arcola.
1797	28	3 May: Arrives in Venice, destroys Venetian Republic. 17 October: Treaty of Campo Formio with Austria, leaving Britain as only enemy. Made commander of the Army of England.
1798	29	Commander of the Army of the Orient. 19 May: Heads for Egypt. 9–14 June: Annexes Malta, reaches Alexandria on 1 July, then, after Battle of the Pyramids on 21 July, reaches Cairo on 24 July.

Year	History	Culture
1794	Execution of Danton. Robespierre's Festival of the Supreme Being. French victory at Fleurus. Thermidor: fall of Robespierre. Habeas Corpus Act suspended in Britain.	Goya, 'Procession of the Flagellants'. Paine, *The Age of Reason*.
1795	French occupation of Amsterdam and annexation of Belgium. Establishment of the Directory. Third Partition of Poland. British occupy the Cape of Good Hope.	Death of James Boswell. Goethe, *Wilhelm Meisters Lehrjahre*.
1796	British occupy island of Elba. Spain declares war on Britain. Death of Catherine the Great of Russia: Paul I becomes Tsar.	Wordsworth, *The Borderers*.
1797	British under Jervis defeat Spanish fleet at Cape St Vincent. Marquis Wellesley (brother of Arthur Wellesley) appointed Governor-General of India.	Coleridge, *Kubla Khan*. Haydn, *Emperor Quartet*.
1798	Nelson destroys the French fleet at Aboukir Bay. Formation of the Second Coalition against France. Rebellion in Ireland. Introduction of income tax as wartime measure in Britain.	Wordsworth and Coleridge, *Lyrical Ballads*.

Year	Age	Life
1799	30	May: Repulse at Acre. 25 July: Victory on land at Aboukir. 23 August: Leaves for France. 9–10 November: Coup d'état of Brumaire creates the consulate, with Napoleon as one of the consuls. Joséphine acquires Malmaison.
1800	31	13 January: Founds the Bank of France. 19 February: Makes the Tuileries palace his official residence. 17 February: Law of 28 Pluviôse establishes prefectorial system. Pacification of the West. 14 June: Napoleon's victory at Marengo. 24 December: Bomb explosion in rue Nicaise – a failed assassination attempt.
1801	32	9 February: Treaty of Lunéville with Austria.
1802	33	27 March: Signs Peace of Amiens with Britain. 18 April: Promulgation of concordat with the Papacy. Becomes Consul for life. Moves out of town residence to palace of St-Cloud.
1803	34	Renews war with Britain. Sells Louisiana to Americans.

Year	History	Culture
1799	Austria declares war on France. Death of George Washington. British in India conquer Mysore.	David, 'Rape of the Sabine Women'. Rosetta Stone discovered.
1800	Moreau's victory at Hohenlinden. British capture Malta.	Schiller, *Mary Stuart*.
1801	French in Egypt surrender to British. Irish Act of Union. Tsar Paul I assassinated: succeeded by Alexander I. Fall of Pitt, succeeded by Addington. Jefferson President of the USA. Nelson defeats the Danes at Copenhagen.	David, 'Bonaparte crossing the Saint-Bernard'. Britain acquires the Rosetta Stone.
1802	France tries to suppress revolt in Haiti.	Chateaubriand, *Le Génie du christianisme*. Denon, *Voyage dans la Basse et la Haute Egypte*. Canova's sculpture 'Napoleon Bonaparte' (now in Apsley House, London).
1803	Arthur Wellesley defeats the Marathas at Assaye in India. Robert Fulton builds first steam-powered boat.	J M W Turner, 'Shipwreck'.

Year	Age	Life
1804	35	Promulgation of the Civil Code. Royalist plot, masterminded by Cadoudal, foiled. 21 March: Execution of the duc d'Enghien. May: Proclamation of the Empire. Napoleon at Boulogne. 2 December: Crowned Emperor in Notre-Dame.
1805	36	26 May: Made King of Italy with Eugène de Beauharnais as Viceroy. 17 October: French victory at Ulm. 2 December: Defeats Austrians and Russians at Austerlitz.
1806	37	Peace of Pressburg with Austria. Makes Joseph Bonaparte King of Naples. Forms the Confederation of the Rhine. Makes Louis Bonaparte King of Holland. 14 October: Defeats Prussians at Jena-Auerstädt. 21 November: Issues Berlin decrees, declaring economic war on Britain. Forms the Grand Duchy of Warsaw. Makes Jérôme Bonaparte King of Westphalia. Starts affair with Maria Walewska.
1807	38	7–8 February: Draws battle of Eylau (against Russia). 14 June: Defeats Russians at Friedland. 25 June: Makes Treaty of Tilsit with Russians. November: French invade Portugal. November, December: Milan decrees tighten economic blockade.

Year	History	Culture
1804	Haiti independent. Lewis and Clarke cross land acquired under Louisiana purchase.	Gros, 'Napoleon at Jaffa'. Beethoven, *Eroica* Symphony.
1805	Third coalition against France formed (Britain, Austria, Russia). 21 October: British fleet wins battle off Cape Trafalgar. Mehmet Ali becomes Pasha of Egypt. Arthur Wellesley resigns in India.	David at work on 'Sacre de Joséphine.' Beethoven, *Fidelio*.
1806	End of Holy Roman Empire. The Holy Emperor Francis II becomes Emperor Francis I of Austria. Death of Pitt leads to formation of Ministry of All the Talents under Grenville. Fox in office for first time since 1784 (dies 1807).	Ingres, 'Napoleon on the Imperial throne'.
1807	British respond to 'Continental System' with Orders in Council. Duke of Portland Prime Minister (till 1809). Miranda and Bolivar start independence movement against Spain. Britain outlaws slave trade.	Lord Byron, *Hours of Idleness*. J M W Turner, 'Sun Rising in Mist'.

Year	Age	Life
1808	39	Establishment of the University of France. April: Meeting with Spanish Bourbons at Bayonne. May: Joseph Bonaparte made King of Spain, Joachim Murat, King of Naples. Spanish rebel. December: Leads brief campaign against British in Spain.
1809	40	British retreat from La Coruña (Corunna). French invade Portugal. After Napoleon is excommunicated, Pius VII is arrested on 6 July and imprisoned. 5–6 July: Defeats Austrians at Wagram. 14 October: Makes peace of Schönbrunn with Austria. 30 November: Tells Joséphine that he will divorce her.
1810	41	Birth of son Alexandre Walewski. April: Marries Marie-Louise of Austria, celebrated at St-Cloud, the Tuileries in the Louvre. Marshal Bernadotte elected Crown Prince of Sweden. Louis Bonaparate ejected from throne of Holland.
1811	42	Year of economic crisis. 20 March: Birth of the King of Rome, later Napoleon 'II'.
1812	43	24 June: Crosses the Niemen to invade Russia. 7 September: Battle of Borodino leads to occupation of Moscow (14 September–14 October). Huge losses during campaign and retreat in Russian winter. 26–28 November: Crossing of the Beresina by retreating French.

Year	History	Culture
_1808_	James Madison President of the USA. Portuguese royal family flees to Brazil.	Canova commissioned to sculpt Napoleon's sister Pauline as 'Venus victrix'. Gros, 'Napoleon at Eylau'. Goya, 'Execution of the Citizens at Madrid'.
_1809_	Ecuador independent of Spain. Spencer Perceval becomes British Prime Minister. Peninsular War: Wellesley defeats French at Oporto and Talavera. Made Viscount Wellington.	Chateaubriand, _Les Martyrs_. Publication of _Description de l'Egypte_ (to 1828).
_1810_	Britain seize Guadeloupe, last French possession in the West Indies. Peninsular War: Wellington victorious at Busaco.	Goya begins 'Disasters of War' series (to 1814). Beethoven, _Egmont_.
_1811_	George Prince of Wales becomes Regent. Mehmet Ali overthrows Mamelukes in Egypt. Pensinsular War: Wellington's victories at Fuentes del Oñoro and Albuera.	Ingres, 'Jupiter and Thetis'. Jane Austen, _Sense and Sensibility_.
_1812_	USA at war with Great Britain (to 1815). Assassination of British Prime Minister Spencer Perceval, succeeded by Lord Liverpool (till 1827), Castelreagh Foreign Secretary (until 1822). Peninsular War: Wellington takes Ciudad Rodrigo and Badajoz, and wins the battle of Salamanca.	Géricault, 'Charging chasseur'. David paints 'Napoleon in his study' for Lord Douglas.

Year	Age	Life
1813	44	Wins battles of Lützen (2 May) and Bautzen (20–21 May). 16–18 October: Is defeated by the allies at battle of Leipzig.
1814	45	Campaign of France. 6 April: Is forced to abdicate. 11 April: allies sign Treaty of Fontainebleau. Exiled on Elba. 29 May: Joséphine dies.
1815	46	1 March: Returns to mainland France in triumph. 'Hundred Days' of rule. 22 April: Restores Imperial Constitution with Acte Additionel. 18 June: Is defeated at battle of Waterloo. Bourbon monarchy is restored for the second time. 15 July: Surrenders to captain of HMS *Bellerophon*. 16 October: Arrives at St Helena. December: After stay at The Briars, moves to Longwood.
1816	47	14 April: Arrival of new governor, Sir Hudson Lowe.
1821	51	5 May: Dies and is buried on the island.

Year	History	Culture
1813	Peninsular War: Wellington defeats Napoleon's brother Joseph at Vittoria and crosses the Pyrenees. Mexico declares itself independent.	Southey, *Life of Nelson* Jane Austen, *Pride and Prejudice*.
1814	September: Start of Congress of Vienna. British burn Washington DC. Treaty of Ghent ends US war with Britain.	David, 'Leonidas at Thermopylae'. Dulwich Picture Gallery opens in London.
1815	Andrew Jackson defeats British at New Orleans. October: Execution of Murat. December: Execution of Marshal Ney.	Scott, *Guy Mannering*. Canova, 'The Three Graces'.
1816	Argentina declared independent. Metternich opens Diet of German Confederation at Frankfurt.	Death of Jane Austen. Constable, 'Flatford Mill'.
1821	Coronation of King George IV.	De Quincey, *Confessions of an Opium Eater*. Constable, 'Hay Wain'.

Further Reading

Primary works

Beside the principal edition of his correspondence referred to in the notes, dating from 1854–70, additional material is available in editions such as that by Frédéric Masson, *Napoléon inconnu* (Paris: 1895). Jean Tulard edited the juvenilia in *Oeuvres littéraires* (Paris: 1968). It is possible to track down issues of the *Bulletin de l'Armée* and the official newspaper, *Le Moniteur*, but usually the reader will find himself confronted with the same passages reproduced in the enormous number of secondary works. It would take many years just to master the memoirs of those who knew Napoleon, from the unreliable recollections of his private secretary Louis Antoine Fauvelet de Bourrienne and of Laura Junot (later duchess of Abrantes) down to the lengthy meditations transcribed by Emmanuel de Las Cases. Fortunately the little book *Napoleon* by the Oxford historian Felix Markham (Weidenfeld & Nicolson, London: 1963) summarises the texts available in English in the 1960s.

Secondary sources

A glance at Frank McLynn's huge bibliography will show how hard it is to master the secondary sources. Among English academic studies of Napoleon some books written in the early 1900s are still worth reading, like the lives by J Holland Rose (1902) and H A L Fisher (1912). From a later generation date lives by H Butterfield (Duckworth, London: 1939), J M Thompson (Blackwell, Oxford: 1952) and Felix Markham, already mentioned. For 35 years Vincent Cronin's elegant *Napoleon* (Collins, London: 1971) has remained in print and shows no sign of losing its appeal, though Frank McLynn's *Napoleon* (Jonathan Cape, London: 1997) matches it in verve, far exceeds it in length and, despite the lack of footnotes, surpasses it in scholarship. Luckily Jean Tulard's masterly discussion of *Napoleon: the Myth of the Saviour* has been translated (Weidenfeld & Nicolson, London: 1984), but those who are set on pursuing his thoughts on the imperial nobility, the coronation, Napoleon's movements, the paintings he inspired, his brother-in-law Murat, the life of the French people under his rule, the reliability of the memorialists of his life, the attempt to assassinate him, his relations with the Vendée or with the composer of the Marseillaise have to be able to read French. Tulard also writes perceptive introductions to the work of fellow historians. There has been no comparable expert on Napoleon and his times since Frédéric Masson a century ago and it is fitting that Tulard is responsible for the *Dictionnaire Napoléon* (Fayard, Paris: 1987).

Among fine popular writers on Napoleon, one who has made himself an expert on the military fortunes of France is Alistair Horne, whose *How far from Austerlitz? Napoleon 1805-15* (St Martin's Press, New York: 1996) is required reading. Corelli Barnett's *Bonaparte* (Allen & Unwin, London: 1978) is pugnacious and critical and takes a line that can be summed up in the title of Owen Connolly's *Blundering to Glory: Napoleon's military campaigns* (Scholarly Resources Inc., Wilmington DE: 1999). Appropriately, two experts on Napoleonic warfare had connections with military academies: John R Elting, author of *Swords around a Throne: Napoleon's Grand Army* (Weidenfeld & Nicolson, London: 1989), and David G Chandler, author of *The Campaigns of Napoleon* (Weidenfeld & Nicolson, London: 1967) and collected essays on the Napoleonic wars (Greenhill Books, London: 1994). It is fascinating to move from Chandler's discussion of Napoleon's attempts at reinventing the course of the battle of Marengo to a study of the sources published by le capitaine de Cugnac, *Campagne de l'Armée de Réserve en 1800,* vol II (Paris: 1900). Such an exercise will show how seldom anyone can be certain that any details of any account of any battle are accurate.

Among standard histories of the period are A Cobban, *A History of Modern France,* vols 1 and 2 (Penguin Books, Harmondsworth: 1957, 1961) and D M G Sutherland, *France 1789-1815* (Fontana Press/Collins, London: 1985). Translated works that deal with internal history are Louis Bergeron, *France under Napoleon* (Princeton University Press, Princeton: 1981), Maurice Guerrini, *Napoleon and Paris* (Walker, New York: 1970) and François Furet, *Revolutionary France, 1770-1880* (Blackwell, Cambridge, Mass.: 1992). Georges Lefebvre's *Napoleon* (Paris: 1963) provides a marvellous panorama of European events seen through the prism of its protagonist's actions as French head of state from 1799 to 1815. Philip Mansel, *The Eagle in Splendour* (George Philip, London: 1987) is excellent on the imperial court. Timothy Wilson Smith's *Napoleon and his artists* (Constable, London: 1996) is an introduction to Napoleon's patronage of the arts and the same author's *Napoleon: Man of War, Man of Peace* (Constable, London: 2002) argues the case for the enduring importance of his reign to France. E E Y Hales had the gift of making church history readable in *Revolution and Papacy, 1779-1846* (Eyre & Spottiswoode, London: 1960) and *Napoleon and the Pope* (Eyre & Spottiswoode, London: 1962).

What attracts most people to the story of his life is the Napoleonic adventure. There is a fluent account of a key episode in J Christopher Herold's sardonic *Bonaparte in Egypt* (Hamish Hamilton, London: 1963). Among recent accounts of the 'Polish war' is a superb narrative by a Pole, Adam Zamoyski's *1812: Napoleon's fatal march on Moscow* (HarperCollins, London: 2004).

English readers who wish to follow the course of the Peninsular War can rely on Elizabeth Longford's *Wellington: Years of the Sword* (Weidenfeld & Nicolson, London: 1969). An ingenious discussion of the relationship between the two men, who never met, can be found in Andrew Roberts's *Napoleon and Wellington* (Weidenfeld & Nicolson, London: 2001). Even after a decade Tom Pocock's *Nelson* (Pimlico, London: 1994) remains one of the best biographies. As with Nelson, Napoleon's love life has attracted a lot of attention and may be traced in Evangeline Bruce, *Napoleon and Josephine: An Improbable Marriage* (Weidenfeld & Nicolson, London: 1995), Alan Palmer, *Napoleon and Marie-Louise* (Constable, London: 2001), and Christopher Hibbert, *Napoleon: his wives and women* (HarperCollins, London: 2002).

Picture Sources

The author and publishers wish to express their thanks to the following sources of illustrative material and/or permission to reproduce it. They will make proper acknowledgements in future editions in the event that any omissions have occurred.

Alinari-Brogi-Giraudon: pp. 2, 9, 18, 22, 26, 35, 58, 61, 68, 93, 97, 99, 112, 133; Getty Images: pp. i, iii, 33, 42, 50, 51, 75, 79, 83, 98, 111, 119, 131, 136.

Index